Ottakar's Local History Series

Burton upon Trent

The changing face of Burton – two postcards from different eras.

Ottakar's LOCAL HISTORY *Series*

Burton Upon Trent

Compiled by
Glenys Cooper

TEMPUS

First published 2001
Copyright © Ottakar's plc, 2001

Ottakar's Local History Series

Produced in association with
Tempus Publishing Limited
The Mill, Brimscombe Port,
Stroud, Gloucestershire, GL5 2QG

ISBN 0 7524 2282 0
Typesetting and origination by
Tempus Publishing Limited
Printed in Great Britain by
Midway Colour Print, Wiltshire

A view of the Old Burton Bridge, now replaced by the Trent Bridge. The building in the centre still stands today, converted into flats.

Contents

Foreword

Being invited to contribute a foreword for this book gives me the opportunity, on behalf of all local historians, to thank Tempus Publishing Limited for their initiative and challenge in promoting this valuable project; Ottakar's Bookstores for their organization and encouragement; and, most importantly, to thank all who have responded and whose contributions make up a splendid addition to the local history record of Burton and District.

It is nearly twenty years since, in association with Richard Farman, I assembled the first picture-history collection that was the first local book of its type to be published. Our seventh volume, next year, will complete a researched archive of over 1,000 images. There is now a great need for new local historians to enter this productive field and to investigate and make available more of the fascinating material that is still around and has not yet been exhaustively studied or published. Stories of many localities, organizations, events and personal recollections await the telling.

It is vital in this rapidly changing era that the facts and memories of the past are chronicled for posterity, both in words and pictures, and I hope that as a result of this commendable project there will be new enthusiasts, of all ages, who will be encouraged to discover the satisfaction and fascination of collecting, researching and recording all aspects of the local history scene.

Geoffrey Sowerby
August 2001

Introduction

When this project to 'write your own history' was first mentioned it sounded like a fantastic idea. It was contrived between Ottakar's and Tempus Publishing. Local history plays an important part in the lives of Burtonians – we just love to reminisce. The hard part was going to be getting you to actually write it down. The first thing to do was to advertise the fact that there was to be a book published, written entirely by yourselves, and also a competition for the three best entries with a prize for the successful entrants. To do this, a large display was put in the front window at Ottakar's. Next came the business of distributing leaflets through every avenue we could find. Hence there were leaflets at the library, Bass Museum, post office, Brewhouse, schools, senior citizens' homes, churches and many more places. We also gave out as many as possible in the shop. The Burton Mail ran a piece about the competition. In conjunction with the library, who are always eager to help, we held a local history morning when the public could come and meet local authors to ask advice or receive help with ideas etc. Thankfully there were enough of you who felt it was a worthwhile project and subsequently sent in your entries. This is where the 'fun' began for me. There were so many entries that I hardly knew where to start. On sifting through the huge mound before me it became apparent that there was a style to almost all of the entries. Therefore a certain 'type' of book revealed itself. This enabled me to discard some pieces of a more serious nature – pieces where the content was excellent, but which were, perhaps, more appropriate to an in-depth history of Burton. Of course every history should have some serious reading but I have kept it to a minimum and in context. Next came the judging. Who else better to judge than our own local authors? A Sunday was spent in Ottakar's reading through the entries and our winners were found. Congratulations to them! The winning entries are marked in the book. It has been a great honour for me to be involved in such a marvellous project and I would like to thank Ottakar's, my employers, for giving me this chance to be involved with the people of Burton who also must be thanked for their efforts to make this book a success.

Glenys Cooper
August 2001

Judging day. From left to right are Richard Papworth, Richard Stone, Colin Kitching and Dave Stacey, in intense concentration. There was a plentiful supply of coffee and snacks during the six-hour session!

Acknowledgements

I would like to express my gratitude to the Burton Mail for their kind permission to reproduce their photographs and to Mr M. Woodcock for his abundant supply.

I would also like to thank our local authors Geoffrey Sowerby, Richard Stone, Mark Rowe, Dave Stacey, Roger Hailwood, Richard Papworth, Colin Kitching, Neil Adams and Holly Ward for their help with the judging or advice and Dennis Stuart for his best wishes; Gill Oliver from the library; Ottakars Manager Marie Smith for allowing me to take on this project and especially Anna Jeffries who has spent endless hours with me as my right-hand man; Lesley, Lou, John, Jane, Andy, Kath, Caroline, Karen, Becky, Charlie and Oliver who have given me complete support. Also a big thank-you to the Burton people who submitted pieces, without whom this book would not have been possible; a huge thank you to Tempus Publishing especially Charlotte who was always at the other end of the phone; and last but not least, my husband Barry, whom I have neglected somewhat this past month and took complete control over his computer. 'You can have it back now, duck.'

CHAPTER 1
Our Town

Drakelow Power Station being built.

How Would You Like to Live in Burton?

My introduction to Burton on Trent took place in Coronation year [1953] when my husband, a quantity surveyor with Sir Robert McAlpine's in London, came home one day and said 'How would you like to live in Burton on Trent?' 'I've never heard of it,' I said. 'Where is it?' 'You'd better find out,' he replied. 'We're moving in a fortnight!' And we did – me, my husband and my three-year-old boy and girl twins. Why did we come? For my husband to build Drakelow Power Station – not single-handed of course; he did have help!

When we moved to Burton we went to live in Stapenhill in Lyndham Avenue, one of the avenues off Clay Street which at that time finished after the GF News shop, but now has almost made a complete new village as Clay Street winds its way up into Brizlincote Valley.

I'm afraid I'm not very technical about the power station because I'm not quite sure of all the details. It seemed to me to be a long time ago, as I'm hoping that somebody will write a real history of Drakelow Power Station to go in with the other histories of Burton. In the '40s the British Electrical Authority asked the council to buy Drakelow Hall and Estate in order to construct the power station on that land. Work on the site began in May 1950 and five years later in November 'A' Station was ready. Sometimes I would push the twins in their pushchair from Stapenhill to Drakelow – quite a push – so that we could see the work in progress and also be entertained by some of the McAlpine Fusiliers, the Irishmen who worked as navvies on the estate. I should say labourers not navvies!

I don't know if the history of Burton changed a great deal with our coming but my history certainly took a turn. I had been used to going to the theatre, cinema, concerts etc. and when I asked where the theatre was in Burton I was told, 'There isn't one.' I was so dismayed I almost went back to London! But in time I found the Little Theatre where I spent many, many, happy hours. That's now gone, of course, with the Drama School.

Now, when 'A' Station was finished McAlpine's didn't intend for the others to be built. My husband moved on to Rotherham to another power station and the twins and I had the opportunity to go back to London. We didn't. They had of course started school so we decided to stay in Burton. I mean, where in London could eight-year-olds see a calf being born as they did at Bailey's Farm? How they loved the springtime when they would go into the wood to pick the little daffodils!

I wonder how many people remember the Boots branch where after shopping we could have afternoon tea in the café, or in the tea bar in Woolworth's? Then there was Stockbridges where the family served with great courtesy and the twins stood on the counter to pull the handle and send the money up the cash desk.

How difficult it is now to remember Burton before Cooper's Square and the Octagon and the bustling busy market days that have so deteriorated. Where did we take the children before McDonald's, where today do four generations of our family meet every week? One of the penalties of age is the loss of memory but thinking hard and talking about things brings back a lot of happiness.

The power station which brought us to Burton suffered a change of appearance in 1997 when in November the boiler house of 'A' Station and in December four cooling towers were demolished. It is a sign of the times that the British Electrical Authority is now called TXU Europe Power with a list of faxes and websites. Far from the old days when you put a shilling in the meter and complained bitterly by telephone, or in person, when something upset the supply!

I look back with great fondness at my years here and am very glad that my husband asked me that day, 'How would you like to live in Burton-on Trent?'

Jeannette Purkiss

Fred's Snippet

Frederick Smith, is ninety-two years of age and has lived in Burton upon Trent all his life. He has many memories, often amusing, and some of them are scattered throughout these pages as Fred's Snippets.

The AA built a horse track around Drakelow Hall but it wasn't a success so the hall was sold and pulled down to make way for Drakelow Power Station.

Newcomer to the Town

I was thirteen years old when I first heard of Burton-on-Trent. My early years had been spent in Mansfield where I passed my days at the Queen Elizabeth Grammar School for Boys and my evenings and weekends were consumed with a passion for football. I was useless at playing the game but since 1966 and all that, I lived for those Saturday afternoons and Monday evenings when Mansfield Town played at home.

When Dad announced that his office was closing and that he would need to find a new job my first fear was this would take us away from 'The Stags'. One or two boys in my class had already left and it always seemed unthinkable that I would be next. I remember Northampton and Chester being discussed, both of whom had teams in the lower divisions of the league but it was Burton-on-Trent whose name cropped up most often. One of the customers with whom my father dealt was keen to rescue his career and it wasn't long before he had accepted a position with Midland Joinery in Lichfield Street. At first he would commute the forty-odd miles. This would take an hour on a good day as he edged around Derby and through Ripley and the streets of Sutton-in-Ashfield. This was 1970 and the A38 that we know today was still some years away.

I recall my first visit to the town. The shopping centre was at least modern, but with sixties concrete and howling gales blowing between the rows of shops it was hardly attractive. I remember standing in the doorways watching the rain pound the paving in the square outside Boots.

I remember driving out to look at the schools. It was assumed that I would transfer to the Boys' Grammar School but when we arrived at the locked gates I could see no goal posts, only the much taller poles that indicated that this was rugby territory. On the spot, I decided that sharing my education with girls was a lesser evil and opted for the Dovecliff Grammar instead.

Home ownership had been for the wealthy in the sixties and we left our council home in Mansfield in November 1971 for a much newer but smaller council house in Burton. At least we were end of terrace and the garage was just a few yards away. (We had a walk of about a quarter of a mile at the old house.)

My first day at school was an interesting experience. I had insisted on starting on a Thursday, reasoning that two days to get acclimatized was better than a whole week. Each move to a new classroom meant a fresh search for a spare seat. All good sport for the other thirty-five students that already knew the ropes.

The second day at school was also memorable for very different reasons. As the old maroon and cream bus pulled up at the bus stop in Waterloo Street, I stepped aboard, ignorant of the local custom of Dovecliff children waiting for the No. 2 while Horninglow pupils boarded the No. 1. The journey to the corner of Beam Hill and Tutbury Road was a raucous initiation into the differences between the then separate schools and I did not make that mistake again!

During those early days the boys gave me a cautious welcome, much amused at my Mansfield Town bag and bemused at the length of my hair, resting as it did on my shoulders. 'You'll have to get that cut once Percy sees it', they warned. I still remember my first meeting with the games master. The crowds parted like the Red Sea before Moses to leave me facing this stocky, white haired, red faced man with bulging eyes that betrayed disbelief at the vision before him.

Unhappily, I agreed to a trim and found a barber in Derby Street, not far from our new home. I have often wondered whether the games master briefed all local hairdressers on his preference for military styling as I can think of no other reason for my request for a 'light trim' producing such a copious pile of cuttings at the foot of the chair.

The girls' welcome was altogether different. It appeared that a competition to be first to 'go out' with the new boy was immediately launched, particularly amongst the girls one or even two years junior to me. If I was flattered I was totally ill-equipped to deal with this unexpected attention and it would be another two years before I was brave enough to be seen with a girl on my arm.

Rolleston Youth Club was the place to go in 1973. Though it was an hour's walk from home, I would make the journey twice a week and again if there was a disco on Saturday night. The top Radio 1 disc jockeys were regularly in attendance, though anyone that remembers those days will always think back to the visit of Johnnie Walker, and what was undoubtedly the first and last Youth Club appearance of his topless dancer, Virginia Plain.

There was not much to do at other times. Summer evenings would be spent on Shobnall playing fields, either kicking a ball around, playing the pitch and putt or kicking our heels on the swings. I might hang around town on a Saturday, on the grass behind the old Woolworth's if the weather was fine. You would usually find somebody you knew there. In the evenings we would make our own entertainment. There seemed to be a lot more house parties than there are now, though from a parent's perspective, I'm in no rush to turn the clock back on that one! Maybe I can remember the state we left some of the houses in too clearly. And why was it always the bathroom mirror that got broken?

Down the road, Derby County were winning League Championships but this was no substitute for Field Mill. To make matters worse, Mansfield fell into a period of decline that saw them relegated after an autumn that saw consecutive 5-0 home defeats and not as much as a goal at home before January. All humiliating stuff for the proud teenager trying to defend his allegiances. I tried 'the Albion', of course. The black and gold stripes were worn proudly at the time, with one of the longest unbeaten runs in Southern League history

My new home team.

underway as I arrived in the town. Russell Bostock was the hero of the day, running the show from midfield while launching regular exocets to warm both the crowds and the fingers of the opposing goalkeeper (if they were lucky!)

Of course, I adopted the giant centre-half, Phil Annable, as my favourite. Running on the pitch after the closing game of the season I called after him to discard his numbered sock-tag for 'a Mansfield fan'.

I judged correctly that his seasons in Mansfield's reserve team without gracing the First XI had not embittered him against his home town team and he stooped to pull open the ties before casting it towards me.

Slowly but surely I began to find my way around the town. I discovered a second-hand record shop near the corner of Station Street where Sainsbury's now stands. I would often stop off on the way home whenever we had had swimming as last lesson. This was always at the old baths, of course, off the old bridge in what looked, felt and often smelt like a brick structure built around a 25-yard stretch of the Trent.

The old library building, on the opposite corner from the record store, suddenly became far more interesting once they started to issue LPs on loan as well as books. And Viking Coaches office, also in the same part of town, became an essential stop off to see which bands were touring. In the early seventies a 'tour' usually gave you a choice of Leicester, Birmingham, Stoke or Stafford, and Viking were the people to get you there.

Before 1950 the team were known as Burton Wanderers. Do you recognize anyone? (M. Wright)

Of course, the golden years are soon gone. For me, discovering Burton between 1971 and 1974 was a parallel exercise to discovering life as my own man. Some will find that sad and I have little doubt that I could have chosen a more glamorous setting for my adolescence.

But memories are not made like that. In November I will have been here for thirty years and many of the friends that I made since arriving are also still in the town. Can't be that bad, can it!

Steve Rhodes

Returning to my Roots

Just prior to leaving school (late 1962), I began to wonder what this great big world, and in particular Burton on Trent, had to offer me. Up to this point I, like many kids of my age at that time, had given little if any thought of a job, let alone a career. At this time jobs were plentiful and one could literally leave one job on a Friday and walk into another the following Monday. Nowadays one leaves a job with little, if any, hope of securing another, notwithstanding the abundance of qualifications one might have.

I could see what was happening in Burton on Trent. It seemed as though everyone's father worked at a brewery – after all we did have a few large ones to choose from in those days, Ind Coope & Allsopp, Bass, Marstons and Everards to name but four. If one was lucky enough to have a relative working at a brewery then the job was all but guaranteed for that person: a job with good pay and security.

Like many in those days I was fortunate

enough to have a father who worked at the brewery (Ind Coope & Allsopp) and so I left school and walked into my first job as a brewery labourer. My father had at one time worked at Marstons and because of his contacts I began my first job there. I can recall that two of my main jobs were cleaning the Unions in the Union room and the other was transporting large bags of flour from a lorry up into the flour room. There were of course other similar jobs during the course of a working day and for a boy of sixteen some of it was, believe me, very hard.

One of my menial tasks every morning was to take my boss his morning allowance of beer and this led to my first brush with music. My boss was Joe Seaman, father of Phil Seaman who was to become a world famous jazz drummer. I met and knew Phil very briefly but unfortunately he died relatively early in his life.

Eventually my father secured for me a better-paid job at Ind Coope & Allsopp and so I then left Marstons and moved to Ind Coope's bottling stores in Curzon Street, which is now the Imex Business Park. I left Marstons on the Friday and started at Ind Coope on the Monday.

At this time I had no real social interests except singing. Albeit in the bath and daily in front of the mirror at home, I would imagine myself as one of the singers I was now seeing and taking an interest in on TV. My interest, however, soon became a passion which I felt I must pursue, and pursue I did, in earnest.

I saw an advert in the Burton *Daily Mail*; a local group was advertising for a singer, 'no experience necessary'. I applied, was auditioned and overnight became Karl Justice of Karl Justice and the Jury. Within six months or so we had our own 2,000-

Tony Mulcahy fronting 'Millennium', at Belvedere Park Club, c. 1997. (B. Higgs)

strong fan club. For a long time I could not believe I was in a 'pop group' and that we had our own fan club, and still only sixteen going on seventeen years of age. We were one of many groups in Burton at that time, and good groups they were. After a while I became very confident and I soon knew what I wanted to achieve and nothing was going to stand in my way. I turned my back on Burton on Trent and left the security of a job and home to see what life had to offer elsewhere. I went to live in Leicester. I had never had to care for myself before, it was strange, it was daunting and it was lonely.

It was whilst living in Leicester, now established and full of confidence, that I was presented with the opportunity of turning professional, my ultimate dream. It was here that I became friends with Mr

Mervyn and Olive Dorsey, the parents of Gerry Dorsey, a.k.a. the famous master of romance, Englebert Humperdinck. Suddenly, I was experiencing a life filled with opportunities which exceeded my expectations and was a far cry from the future I had faced only a couple of years before back in Burton on Trent. I took up the opportunity of turning professional and was soon travelling and singing in countries that I had only ever heard of, and was appearing with, and meeting socially, pop icons I had previously only worshipped and admired from afar. Sadly due to a serious accident in 1973 all this came to end and my bubble burst.

I returned to Burton on Trent in 1974 on my GP's advice, 'temporarily', and I have remained here ever since. I was unable to

Rolling the barrels at Ind Coope.

pursue a singing career for some eighteen months after my return and eventually when I did so it was only as a sideline in addition to working at a 'normal' job again. When living in Leicester I attended Leicester University for a short while studying law. Why law? I don't know, but the interest rekindled when I returned to Burton on Trent.

After I returned it was clear that the secure jobs had all but disappeared and people were no longer rushing to work at the breweries. All those friends, family and relatives that were all working at the breweries when I left were married, raising a family and still working at the brewery.

The drug scene was always prevalent and sadly I saw two very good friends of mine lose their lives as a result. It was seeing the not so healthy in the early 1970s that made me decide to try and help in some small way and so for three or four years I occasionally helped raise money for the physically and mentally handicapped in Burton on Trent.

In 1991 I began in earnest to assist cancer patients because this dreadful disease almost took away someone very dear and close to me. I have raised money for cancer patients in various ways during the last ten years. For example, a Land's End to John O'Groats hike, annual live '60s music events, annual quiz nights and a free-fall parachute drop.

All the money I have raised to date has been given to our own cancer unit at the Queen's Hospital here in Burton on Trent for the treatment of cancer patients. Burton on Trent is of course the town I once left but returned to 'temporarily' back in 1974.

Tony Mulcahy

Fred's Snippet

There used to be a job at the breweries called 'knocker-up'. It was his job to go round on his bike in a morning and wake up the shift by tapping on their windows with a long cane or by throwing small pebbles which he carried in his pocket. Each brewery had a buzzer which sounded at the start of a shift. You had to have your 'tally' on its peg by then or you lost time. Each buzzer had a different tone so you knew which brewery it was. The buzzers were sounded by letting out steam in the boiler rooms. The deepest sound came from the Branston Factory hooter which was off one of the well-known steam ships.

Town Centre Living

I came to live in Burton on Trent in the fifties when there was hardly any accommodation to rent so I bought a small cottage in the centre of town with one bedroom, a living room, a scullery and an outside toilet. There was one cold water tap and a gas supply, no electricity. A regular supply of gas mantles for lighting was essential as these were very fragile and the living room ceiling was very low. Tall people tended to set their hair alight when they stood up!

Flat irons were not an ornament but an essential piece of equipment. There was an iron grate complete with oven, which was all I had to cook on initially, but I soon installed a gas stove. Water had to be

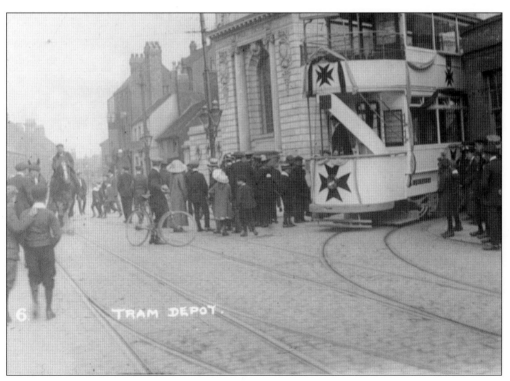

A tram leaving the depot in Horninglow Street.

heated to wash clothes and dishes and bath night was a lengthy affair due to the need to boil saucepans of water to fill the tin bath. The scullery doubled as a bathroom and the water was tipped out of the back door afterwards. Fortunately there was a launderette nearby which was a great help in the winter or when it rained.

I used a bicycle to go to work but as there was so little space inside the house I had to leave it outside. One night I forgot to bring it inside and during the following night someone threw it onto the nearby railway track. This was in the days when brewery trains crisscrossed the town, with level crossings where the railway line passed over a street. The first train in the morning drove straight over my bike which must have been a nasty shock for the driver who had no way of knowing, in the dark, what he had hit! Vandalism is nothing new.

After two years I was informed by the housing department of the council that my house was condemned as unfit for habitation because of the lack of facilities and I was allocated a nice new council house. Naturally I was happy to have hot water, a bathroom and plenty of space but

The game shop in the High Street.

Station Street. The crossing gates and old house have since been demolished to make way for Worthington Way.

I had enjoyed living in my cosy cottage. I still have my flat iron but nowadays it is only used as a door stop.

I feel closer to the past for having faced up to the challenge of living without labour-saving devices and, while I would not be without a television, much of the entertainment provided is not worth watching. The library, then situated in Union Street, was, and still is, my main source of enjoyment and in the summer there were the lovely riverside walks.

Burton has changed immeasurably over the last fifty years but it will never lose its unique character. The market was the main focus for shopping on Thursdays and Saturdays which accounts for the number of people who still go into town on a Thursday though not for the market to the same extent. Wednesday was early closing day and no one dreamt that there would be shops open on Sundays as there are now.

Although I thought Burton was quaint and charming at the time I must admit that I am happier to have all the modern shops and transport to get to them, especially as I am fifty years older than I was then.

Mary Smith

The brewery trains were unique to Burton and there were sixty-two crossings over the roads in town, so you did not have to go very far before you came to a crossing. The crossings had big white gates with a notice on which said 'when the bell rings these gates will open'. Now, when I went to town with my mother she always seemed to be in a hurry, and if the bell rang at one of these crossings, she would tell me to hurry up. I would either linger or pretend my shoelace had come undone so that I could stand at the closed gates and wave at the train and engine driver. I always got a wave back. I thought it was worth a bit of a telling-off by my mother. A fine example of this railway network and a model of the town can be seen at the Bass Museum. (Keata Edwards)

Burton Shops

My first recollection is going to live down Dale Terrace. There were ten houses and we lived at No. 6. The houses were owned by Mr Newton Husbands who lived at Branston. We had to go down an opening to get to Dale Terrace and I think it was called Kottingham Works, well I am sure of it. The works were something to do with the brewing trade – yeast merchants. I was only a child but I can remember the brick building at the side as we went down the opening. At the back of our house there was another yard, called Slater's Yard. We used to climb over the wall to get over, and it brought you out in Moor Street. There was a shop on the corner of Alfred Street, called Simnett and Harris which was a grocer's, and you could take a bottle for wine, or whatever, loose. On the other corner was the Builders Arms, which is still there under another name. Times were hard then. My dad was out of work for years, my mother was on the means test. She got two shillings for me, the eldest child, as there were three of us at that time in the late twenties and early thirties. Kottingham Works was only pulled down this year, and it is now part of a garage. Across the road in Dale Street was the Derbyshire Farmers, a milk place, and at the side was Anglesey Road railway line. My mother used to take us there to see the trains go by; it was a real treat. In those days, cows used to go in the street and as we were living down an opening, the cows got out of hand and would go down the yard and be outside our houses. I used to be frightened to death, seeing them outside the door. The houses were only two up and two down and a washhouse outside combining a toilet.

I remember New Street: Gibson's on the corner, the chemist; Jefferson's the grocers next door; and a little shop, Foden's, where my dad always bought his caps, and the men's toilet urinal which is now at Bass's Museum. Further on were Miss Christian at the sweet shop and Mr Ives the jeweller, the Infirmary where you could go to out-patients and get help for any accident or wound. Trigg's toffee shop near the Infirmary – they made home made sweets, toffee fishes, what a treat! The Derby Telegraph was on the corner of Union Street, and the New Street Baptist church, which I remember burned down. There was a little Chapel in Dale Street also. I remember Bill Ash the butcher. There were three grocers' shops also in Dale Street, with Mrs Roper on one corner. Godfreys, then Miss Chapmans when they left, were on the corner of

Moor Street low bridge in 2000. It has now been pedestrianized. The slope in the left-hand corner was the ramp to the level crossing for high loads. (T.H. Hines)

Paget Street, and Bells on the other corner opposite Ropers. Going back to New Street, there was Joyce the antique shop at the top end. No one could afford antiques in those days. The fruit market was down an opening. Miss Chapman ran a second hand shop, with clothes right to the top of the ceiling. My mother gave me sixpence to go and get a coat when I was about ten years old, and she (Miss Chapman) pulled one out and gave it to me. Didn't have to be proud in those days. At Parsons sweet shop there was lovely ice cream if you could afford one. There was always a fish and chip shop across the road, also a shop that did the steam laundry, which was situated in Watson Street, employing lots of women. That was hard work in those days. I haven't any pictures – only happy memories of things and places gone forever. I am now eighty-one, eighty-two in October. I was born in Burton, went to Christ Church School, then won the eleven-plus and went to Broadway Central School, which is now Branston Court.

Margaret Dawson

High Street, showing tramlines, bicycles and carriages.

CHAPTER 2
Boyhood Memories

Horninglow St John's Peace Tea.

Horninglow

I was born in Horninglow where I spent most of my early life. My actual place of birth was in Loverocks Yard, which was opposite Mr Brooks' farm (he was later to become Alderman Brooks). In the yard were twelve small cottages, a pump outside for water and two pan toilets for the twelve houses. If you had fallen out with the neighbours, and you needed to use the toilet

it was 'hard lines', they would stay there all night!

Wash day was every Monday, with the copper in the back kitchen and the mangle and the dolly tub outside. There were fire grates with a boiler at the side and ovens that were used for cooking everything. These ovens had shelves that came out and we would wrap a towel around them and take them to bed to keep warm. The straw mattresses on the bed were hard as iron.

Miss Forbes kept a small shop across the road from our house. One day she said she had found some old hair oil, a penny a bottle if you took your own bottle. I bought some but when I came to use it, it was missing. When I asked my mother where it was she had oiled the mangle with it. Mr Hadfield was our barber, and would only cut hair on Saturday when he came home from work at Bass's. We had to sit on the floor in the back yard. Mr Oliver Stevens who lived in Horninglow Road was the local blacksmith, fireman and preacher. I never saw him without his bowler hat. He even wore it when he shod the horses. Mrs Pountney was the midwife and 'layer out' in Horninglow. She was a very big woman who rode a three-wheeler cycle. Mr Bradbury used to hire out cycles and although he was totally blind he could mend any cycle. Mr Forbes was the landlord of the Gate Inn; he was also the undertaker. He used to make the coffins and we always knew if someone had died by the sounds of sawing wood and hammering. His son Harry was the local milkman and his other son was the first in the area to have a taxi.

Harry Bindley was a regular in the Royal Marines. If he was on leave at the time of the Gate picnic he caused chaos. Once he took a party of locals to go and see Derby County and on the way they called at every pub between the Gate and Derby Turn. At Derby Turn Mr Leedham had a cab stand. They asked him to take them to Derby. Now Mr Leedham was a clean-living man and objected to their swearing and noise, so, he took the horse out of the shafts and left them there. It was sometime before they realized that they hadn't moved. When Harry went back from leave, his pals went to see him off at the station and called at all the usual pubs on the way. When the train came in they all got on and the train went off. In the end the police called to put the wives minds at rest. The men were miles away.

During the school holidays, we made good use of leisure time. A group of us hired a tent for 5s a week from 'Ropey Wrights'. We camped in what used to be Pinfold Lane (now Kitling Greaves). Our parents saw little of us during that month. We lived on bird's eggs, rabbits, turnips and anything else that was going! We drank spring water. There was a very docile cow in the next field, and we used to milk her into a teapot. We often wondered if the farmer thought it strange if the cow was dry.

The outdoor sport was mostly football and one of my older brothers played football for Horninglow village team. On one occasion one of the team was getting married at Horninglow Chapel. The rest of the team waited for him to come out of chapel and then carried him off as they were a man short! Us youngsters formed our own football teams, made our own goal posts and fetched sawdust in a barrow from Kind's to mark out the pitch. No one could afford a full kit in those days.

On the way to school we used to play marbles in the gutter and at night we played games – snakes and ladders, draughts, and Meccano if anyone owned one. The other games we played were whip and top, marbles, wooden hoops and clappers (two bones).

Our first wireless was home-made. It was a crystal set and when trying to tune it you had a 'cats-whisker' to find the station you wanted. London used to be '2LO London calling'. We had to have a large pole in the garden 20 or 30ft high for the aerial.

We in Tutbury Road had a well-known boxing family by the name of Mayns. George was the light heavyweight champion of Burton; Alf, his brother, was heavyweight champion and Ted was lightweight champion of Burton. They taught us how to look after ourselves, which we did! There was a big fight in Burton when George fought another well-known boxer, Billy Jordan. Before another big fight in Burton George had arranged a boxing match between some South Derbyshire lads and us Horninglow lads. I was one of them. We drew names from a hat to see who would fight each other. I drew against a youth called 'Battling Bates' from Swadlincote. I had not seen him before we got in the ring, we were the same height but he was cross-eyed in both eyes and he mesmerized me! I did not last long and that was the end of my boxing days! All I got was a good hiding and two shillings for the night.

Opposite the chapel was a two-storey building known as the Scout room. The lower floor was used for dancing and the top floor as a shooting range. Mr Simnett and Mr Richardson used to show lantern slides there to people wishing to emigrate to Canada, New Zealand and Australia. In those days a farm worker and his family could go for £2. They could get their photographs from Mr Simnett and their passports from Mr Richardson at Nixon's Shipping Office.

There were no buses in those days so we would walk to Tutbury Castle for a day out. The Gate Inn organized a day trip every year. They travelled by a horse-brake owned by Mr Rusconi. There was usually a fight when they arrived home at night but by morning they would all be pals again. The next day was Sunday and food left over from the picnic was finished off in the croft at the back of the Gate. Pillow fights were held and a greasy pole put up with a leg of mutton at the top. The first to climb the pole won the leg of mutton. The only time we came into Burton was to visit Pipers Penny Bazaar, to spend what little money we had.

Horninglow Flower Show was held each August bank holiday Monday in Brooks' field in Rolleston Road. They were keen gardeners in Horninglow and put on a lovely show of flowers and vegetables.

A ceremony called the 'Blessing of the Crops' was held in September, and was a big occasion in Horninglow. The procession would leave the church led by the Salvation Army band, the choir, churchwardens, Sunday school children, Boy Scouts etc. and headed for 'Skippers Hills' where the service was held.

Burton 'Statutes' Fair was another big occasion (and still is). Several fortune-tellers used the shop doorways in New Street to set up their booths. A few years ago I was walking along New Street when one shouted, 'How are you, Fred?' He was calling himself Professor Leo. He went to Horninglow School when I did.

Archie Blankley delivered fish around Horninglow and finished his round at the Gate Inn. What he had left, he would give away. We often had some. There was a lady called Mrs Trowell who used to deliver milk on her round on an upright bicycle. When she was ninety years old they asked her what she would like for her birthday and she said 'a new cycle'

Polly Ford lived on the corner of Pinfold Lane (now Kitling Greaves). She had a croft down the lane and used to wear men's boots and smoke a clay pipe. She was a tough one! She got married late in life to a man she met at the cattle market in Derby Street. I met her about a week later and said, 'How's

Canada Wants Settlers

Special Fares From £2 By Cunard Liners For Approved Settlers

EMPLOYMENT ASSURED

FAMILIES WITH FARMING EXPERIENCE (FREE PASSAGE FOR CHILDREN UNDER 17 YEARS)

MARRIED COUPLES

WOMEN HOUSEHOLD WORKERS

BOYS (FREE PASSAGE IF UNDER 17)

YOUTHS & SINGLE MEN (WILLING TO WORK ON THE LAND)

APPLY NOW FOR SPRING SAILINGS

CALL AT THE PREMISES OF

NIXON'S SHIPPING OFFICE,

Cunard Line Agent,

1, UXBRIDGE STREET, BURTON-ON-TRENT,

ON THURSDAY, NOVEMBER 17TH,

BETWEEN 3 P.M. AND 5 P.M., AND 6 P.M. AND 8 P.M.

A REPRESENTATIVE OF THE CUNARD LINE WILL BE IN ATTENDANCE FOR THE PURPOSE OF GIVING ADVICE TO ALL INTERESTED.

A magic lantern slide shown by Mr Simnett and Mr Richards to encourage farm workers to emigrate to Canada. (F. Smith)

married life, Polly? She said ' I've chucked him out, he said he suffered with rheumatics but he didn't; he had a wooden leg!'

There was a man called 'Salty' – he used to carry a big lump of salt under his arm. If you wanted any he would cut some off. He used to scrape the salt up and down the entries as he walked so you could always follow his trail.

I remember many shops in the Horninglow area. Mrs Harvey was on the corner of Field Lane, this business was later to be bought by my sister Fanny. Mrs Wibberly was at the top of Calais Hill and Mr Goodwin the grocer was on the corner of Dover Road. The Misses Tunley had shops next door to each other, the first sold everything and the second just sold tobacco and sweets. There was Norton's the butchers, the post office kept by Mrs Dorrie, and the Co-op on the corner of Wyggeston Street. Across the road was Russell's a greengrocer. Moving up to the canal basin was Baldock's (where we got our rations), Mark's the haberdasher and Rains who ran a corn merchants.

When the First World War broke out I was five years old. During those war years life was very hard. My first recollection of the war was putting up blackout curtains and having a paraffin lamp for lighting. The winter nights used to be very long with only candles and gas or paraffin lamps for light. When we had an air-raid warning, someone used to run up Horninglow shouting, 'Lights out, Zepps are coming'. Outside our house was a gas lamp. If anyone was able to climb up and put it out, OK; if not, a brick was thrown at it.

I have seen women walking round the streets looking for nub ends of Woodbine cigarettes; they were the cheapest at five for twopence. Horninglow was a very small community but every morning Sir William Bass used to ride through on horseback. He would smoke a cigar whilst riding which he used to throw away when he'd finished, and towards the end there was often quite a scramble for it. We all had a bucket and shovel to collect his horse droppings, and those from the brewery horses – we used to get a penny a bucketful from the gardeners.

One year there was an epidemic of influenza in Burton and scores of people died. Other common diseases were diphtheria, measles, TB and fevers. If you caught any of these, a big white van used to come and take you up to the Fever Hospital at Lower Outwoods. Mr Hadfield (the previously mentioned barber) who lived on the bank was also a 'quack doctor'. (The houses are now demolished.) He used to make an ointment for people who suffered from ulcers and boils. We used to collect large snails for him; if we found a lot he would give us a penny. All we ever found out was that he used to mix the snails with home-cured lard. He also made a stick like a pencil to use on cracks and cuts on the hand. Both were a sure cure. There were many other 'cures' for minor ailments. If you had a sore throat an old sweaty sock would be around your neck, and a bad chest would have been rubbed with goose grease. Nits or head lice would mean having home-cured lard applied to your hair. All bedrooms had a 'po' under the bed and when people had chilblains they'd soak their feet in them. Aching joints would have white oils rubbed into them. These were horse-oils which farmers used on their horses! For earache it was recommended that you put a small warm onion in your ear and then lie on it.

The fire tender was kept in a wooden hut behind Horninglow Institute. It was a large churn between two iron wheels, with a stand pump on top. The hose was fixed in before the churn was filled with water by hand. Once one of Brooks' hayricks caught fire. They rushed in, filled the churn and started to pump. Water went everywhere! Rats had gnawed through the hose.

Situated at the corner of Field Lane was a horse trough, where gypsies met to water their horses. Once a fight broke out and one of the gypsies hit Bill Hanstey in the head with his belt. Bill was carried into our house where my mother took off his boots. It was always said, 'Never die with your boots on'. He died later but they never caught the guilty man.

All these people and incidents stick in my memory and it is with pleasure I recall them.

Frederick Smith
Prize Winner

Fred's Snippet

In those days you always had a Sunday suit. For each year's Sunday School Anniversary you would have a new suit. Most people had their frocks made by a dressmaker. Stokes was a boot repairer on Calais Hill. He would keep the nails in his mouth. They were very small. I don't know if he ever swallowed any.

On the Level

Tell virtually anyone from Winshill that you were brought up 'on the level' and they will know you aren't trying to convince them of your honesty or integrity or, indeed, that of your parents either. What you are actually saying is that most of, if not at all, your formative years were spent living in a house

The magic lantern used by Mr Simnett and Mr Richards (F. Smith)

Fishing on the weir at Rolleston-on-Dove.

along Bearwood Hill Road. Yes, for Bearwood Hill Road read the Level, that long, flat stretch of road running from the top of Bearwood Hill itself all the way to the bottom of Church Hill Street.

With its neat rows of modest terraced houses interspersed by a few slightly grander properties and a scattering of good old-fashioned shops catering for the day-to-day needs of the surrounding population on the face of it the Level could be any street on the edge of town. No, at first glance, there would have appeared nothing particularly special at all about it and that's probably still the case today for it seems to have changed little over the years. But first impressions are often misleading.

Over the years many a weary traveller making their way up Bearwood Hill either by foot or on a bicycle has been mightily relieved to get to the top and see the Level stretching into the distance. Only the fittest cyclists or the lucky ones with lightweight racing bikes with plenty of gears were likely to make it all the way to the summit without getting off part way up and walking the steepest section.

I suppose the hub of the street was the row of shops about half-way along which catered for virtually all our daily requirements. There was a choice of two butchers' shops: Harold Lowndes ran one; Charlie Carter the other. We only went to Carter's but I never found out why. In any case both are long since gone. Excellent fish and poultry came from Sims', also, sadly, no more. Sweets, newspapers and delicious home-made ice cream came from Frank and Mildred Caulton's general store. My shopping list there usually included a packet of '7 o'clock' razor blades and a tin of Four Square pipe tobacco both for my dad and the occasional packet of ten Woodbines – I wonder where they went! You got fruit and vegetables from Baker's the greengrocer and a choice of two chemists, Parry's or Simnett's in those days. And if you needed a quick haircut you could pop into Gibbs' barber's shop. Situated on the other side of the road was Pearson's the gents' outfitters and the ladies could buy a new dress from Fisher's who sold wool for knitting and materials for embroidery – so I'm told. Bert Lowndes, brother of butcher Harold delivered fresh milk from his own cows or you could collect in a jug straight from the cooler. And for the keen angler there was a chap called Albert Baldock who made fishing rods. What more could you possibly need?

Yes, I was brought up on the Level; in fact I lived there from 1943 when I was born until my early twenties in a small terraced house, about half-way along right next door to another business run by the Caulton family – a thriving builder and undertaker. What happy times they were. Weekdays in our house invariably began with the piercing sound of the circular saw from the joiner's shed situated just a few yards from the bottom of the garden. Better than any alarm clock! The joiners always seemed to be busy, with no shortage of customers for the end product of their work – as I said, it was an undertaking business. One day – I would be about ten years at the time – a joiner called Norman decided it would be a good idea to sit me on the workbench, insert my short trousers into the vice, turn it up as tightly as possible and leave me there for an hour or so while he went away to do something else. Very funny in hindsight but not at the time – I've always kept well clear of vices since!

As for Bearwood Hill Road itself, or to be more accurate underneath it, things weren't quite right. In fact there must have been something seriously wrong with the drains to be precise, because whenever there was a severe downpour, and there seemed to be plenty of those, the street would suddenly become a raging torrent as water flooded down from the higher parts of Winshill. What fun it was for a ten-year-old sitting in the front room watching a No. 3 or 4 maroon corporation bus go past the window washing the flood water onto the pavement and into the cellars.

Ah yes, the front room! That rather special place reserved mainly for entertaining visitors for tea, usually on a Sunday, and for parties, particularly birthdays, and of course Christmas. As for the cellar, most houses on the Level had one. Most would be well stocked with coal but some, like ours, were more an Aladdin's cave stacked with jars of home-made pickles and jam, boxes of apples too, as well as the usual assorted bric-à-brac including the odd gas mask left over from the war. Best of all though, bottles of home-made ginger beer at the time when producing your own from a ginger beer plant had become something of a craze. And what a heavy responsibility it was when my dad told me to look out for the coalman! As soon as he arrived my job was to sit in that front room and count the bags as they were tipped into the cellar via the hole on the pavement. One, two, three … sixteen, seventeen – or was it eighteen? Oh dear, lost count again.

Not all the houses on the Level had bathrooms – nothing wrong with a tin bath in front of a roaring coal fire. But we were lucky. Years earlier a spare bedroom had been fitted with a proper bath. The only problem was there was no hot running water so instead we heated up the water in the boiler downstairs in the kitchen and pumped it by hand into the bath. I can still hear that squeaking pump. As for the toilet, just a short walk into the yard. No problem at all except when it froze up during one of those grim winters when even the paraffin lamp wasn't man enough to ward off Jack Frost.

Most of the lads who lived on the Level were keen on football and cricket. Where better to hone our skills in the evenings and during school holidays than in Caulton's brickyard, a flat piece of land covered in gravel surrounded by garages and workshops for the tradesmen? 'Eh you lads, clear off and play somewhere else.' That was the boss himself, Harold Caulton, when he was in a bad mood, although, to be fair, he had been known to join in occasionally. Understandable though – not only were there half a dozen lads playing football or cricket on his property but the chances were that a couple of his tradesmen had decided to down tools to take part as well; much more fun than plumbing, painting or even making coffins. Definitely not what Harold was paying them for, anyway. Early evening we would troop back home faces covered in dust just in time for a quick wash before the signature tune for *Dick Barton* or *Journey into Space* came over the airwaves.

Yes, it was the boys who were playing. Girls could have been living on a different planet as far as we were concerned, they came along a few years later. Cricket was usually played with a tennis ball and over the years we must have lost hundreds of them as they disappeared over garages into something resembling a jungle. In the late autumn when the grass was dying off and the nettles had lost their sting some of us would venture into the undergrowth to search for them – successfully usually. Occasionally a good straight hit and the ball would sail over Harold's office and right across the road eventually thudding against the front of Fisher's shop – that's if it hadn't collided with a passing cyclist, bus or the occasional car!

The sporting seasons were clearly defined. Football usually finished on the day of the Cup Final when everyone rushed out seconds after the final whistle doing their best to emulate the feats of Stanley Matthews or Jackie Milburn. The goals were usually the doors of a garage and the ball could be anything from a tennis ball to a worn out leather football – if we were lucky. Soccer didn't kick off again until the following September. In between cricket – not golf, not tennis, not squash – just cricket.

At the top of the brickyard there were some allotments and a large orchard and behind them, a small piece of relatively flat grassy land surrounded by steep banks which we called the clayhole. To us it was a sort of miniature Wembley Stadium. It must have been from there that clay had been extracted years earlier for making house bricks, hence the name brickyard. I must admit that the allotments were of little interest although most of us had to do a bit of digging or weeding from time to time. As for the orchard, well that was sheer paradise. Apples of course but plenty of pears, plump juicy plums too, and if that wasn't enough there was the odd gooseberry and blackcurrant bush too.

So what were the other highlights for youngsters growing up on the Level? It doesn't seem to have changed a lot over the years and some of the people who lived there when I was growing up still do. Sadly though, the brickyard and the clayhole are long gone – there's a small estate there now – and our house has become part of the run-down DIY shop next door, the front door and window bricked up. Not much chance of sitting in the front room watching maroon double decker buses splashing their way through the floods these days. In any case they've probably sorted out the drains by now. Probably.

David Moore
Prize Winner

Gorby's Knob

They named it Gorby's Knob,
But that's now ancient history.
'Twas long before the birth
Of such delights as you and me.
To us it was Old Winshull,
Though that too's a bygone day;
Environmental progress came
And blasted it away.

The kerbstones where we chewed our crusts,
The pavements where we played,
The backyards where our rabbits lived,
And catapults were made,
The quiet lanes and meadows
Where our early years were spent,
Were bulldozed out of site
By scheduled re-development.

TRENT BRIDGE, BURTON-ON-TRENT.

The Swan Junction before major redevelopment.

Now thinking back we find
The years have hurtled by too fast.
What seems like only yesterday
Is half a lifetime past.
Joey Neal with fruit and veg,
Old Salty with dray;
Paddling in Cherra brook;
The paddocks' new-mown hay.

Miss Tomlinson's for savoury ducks;
Every Tuesday night
Crowding in the Gullet
For another schoolboy fight.
Buying sweets with foreign coins
At Johnny Massey's shop.
Bretby Woods at Whitsuntide;
Cold tea and nettle pop.

The newt pond and the Muckruck,
Pony field, and Kenty's bull.
Scrumping in the orchard;
Stumbling home, all pockets full.
Bobby Chidlow, Sergeant Hill,
The awesome Parson Price.
Choir practice winter nights,
With feet as cold as ice.

Dark lane field – The Peasles
For long strolls on summer nights,
Tails of spaced-out newspaper
On stout brown-paper kites.
Cutting lethal peashooters
From Kedlocks hollow stalks.
Vases filled with totty-grass
Brought home from Sunday walks.
Sound yer Oller, Kick the Tin,
Allerky, and Tip Tap.
Skimming-on, with faggies,
Birds eggs hidden in your cap.

Pockum, Bordo, Jack and Peter,
Arther, Vic, Nimrod,
Perce, Tom, Reg and Ernie,
And the two Rays, Boam and Todd.
Faces, voices, incidents,
At home, at school, at play,
Memories from childhood,
Vividly recalled today.

Herbert Dutton

The Wreck

I always knew it as 'the Wreck'. It never occurred to me that it could ever be called anything else, or even that the Wreck was actually a shortened form. It was only many years later that it dawned on me that the Wreck was short for 'Recreation' and that the Wreck was properly called 'Anglesey Road Recreation Grounds'. Somehow the Wreck seemed more appropriate.

As I was growing up in the 1950s, the Wreck was the place to gather, to play, to walk dogs and to train spot, if you belonged to that earnest brotherhood whose greatest excitement was to enter numbers in a well-thumbed notebook, as one of the steam-wreathed monsters flashed past.

The railways were an integral part of the Wreck. The Leicester line ran over the bridge that formed the entrance to the Wreck and the main Birmingham line formed the southern boundary. To the east were the Wagon Works and the western border was formed by some allotments. Train spotters traditionally gathered by a sort of stile in the far corner by the allotments, an excellent place to view the trains as they pulled out of Burton station, or were shunted to the loco sheds a little further down the line toward Oxford

Street. Each train that passed would set off knowledgeable discussions in the pseudo-scientific jargon beloved of small boys about bogeys and wheel formations, along with frantic scribbling of the all-important engine number. None of it made any sense to me. I just stood there in a mixture of fear and wonder as we were engulfed in a cloud of steam, smoke, noise and earth-trembling vibration.

To enter the Wreck you first had to work your way down Cambridge Street, past a quiet row of houses (for whose residents the endless procession of boys kicking footballs or larking about on bikes must have been a constant trial), past Scrappy Moore's scrap heap to the left and some toilets on the right, then under the Leicester line bridge into the Wreck itself. The toilets must have been built in a moment of council-inspired optimism, only ever to be used in extremis, and only then if you could hold your breath for up to two minutes. I don't ever recall there being a supply of running water, except for the occasional steady stream issuing from burst pipes.

Under the Leicester Line Bridge were a series of hazards for the unwary. Frequently flooded, not just by the toilets, and then only passable by a precarious tightrope walk along a narrow shelf of raised bricks. Puddles filled the potholes even on the driest of days and the whole area was strewn with half-bricks and broken glass. One of my earliest memories

Entrance to the Wreck in 2000. (P. Whiteland)

is of falling down under the bridge whilst walking the dog with my Mum, and cutting my forehead open on a jagged piece of glass. The unexpected benefit of this trauma was a cross-shaped scar on my forehead, which left me with messianic tendencies that took a while to shake off (the lack of disciples was a bit of a giveaway).

Having made your way under the bridge, you could either go straight on and join the train-spotting tendency or climb the side of the ramp leading from the Leicester line and survey the whole of the Wreck. This was a good vantage point. From here you could spot friends, enemies, games in progress, dogs to avoid and the current usage of the recreational facilities. These consisted of a set of swings, a roundabout of the sort that resembled an upside down shuttlecock balanced on a pole and a further roundabout which was a solid wooden structure about four feet high with metal handles. All of these were potential death traps in the hands of the psychotically exuberant, of which there were more than a few. To the right of this feast of amusement was a large, brick-built, shed-like structure with a tarmac-covered forecourt. The shed was open along the side facing the Wreck. I could never understand its intended purpose. Presumably the Council saw it as a rather Spartan changing room. At one time wooden benches had run along the walls, but these had long since fallen victim to the vandals who inhabited the Wreck in the darkness of the night. In reality, it formed an uncomfortable shelter in the driving rain for the disparate groups that shared the Wreck. It was often a home of passion and covert drinking as night fell,

and a place for those with even less wholesome interests to lurk.

From your vantage point at the top of the ramp you might spot the telltale signs of a prospective football match. Jackets or jumpers strewn about an area whilst a group of lads argued heatedly about the correct dimensions of their chosen area of competition. I always hated football. Not playing, of course, was not an option, even though I was useless. You waited while the captains (who always seemed to be self-elected) chose their teams one by one from the assembled ranks. I was usually the last to be chosen and, sometimes, an argument would break out between the captains as to who was to have the ultimate handicap of me on their team. Eventually the game would begin. Nowadays every child seems to be a budding professional and have a clear grasp of tactics and strategy. In those days the favoured formation was the 'flying wedge'. This worked as follows. The player with the ball (usually the captain; after all, it was his ball) would set off down the field, dribbling the ball, with the rest of his team in hot pursuit behind him, in a sort of wedge-shaped formation. Those who had the least desire to actually come into contact with the ball (i.e. me) hurtled along at the back of this wedge, all strenuous effort and enthusiasm, without ever contributing anything to the game. The worst scenario was if evening was beginning to fall and one of the parents came over to see where we were, and then decided to join in. If my luck ran true to form, it would be my dad, fresh from the pub and convinced of his own sporting prowess. One or two of the most able of our group would attempt to tackle him and, sometimes, (having the advantage of

A view from the ramp. (P. Whiteland)

sobriety) succeed. I would try to blend into the background, consumed by embarrassment and ineptitude.

Alternatives to football, depending on the season, were cricket (proper or French if no one had any equipment other than a tennis ball and a piece of wood), tick, illurky 1-2-3 (don't ask: I can't remember what it involved, although I think it was a variation of hide and seek), running, bike scrambles, sledging, go-karting (pram wheels and odd arrangements of scrap wood being the principal ingredients) and building forts/dens either from old tyres or hay, or both. The tyres came from the scrap-yard. Great, heavy lorry tyres retrieved at considerable risk from the haphazard piles of old cars, prams and other junk that constituted the scrap-heap. We were always

acutely aware that we could be caught at any moment and yet I can never recall seeing anyone working on the piles of scrap, nor, for that matter, can I remember seeing anyone bringing scrap to the yard or taking it away other than us. The tyres would be rolled under the bridge, over the ramp and onto 'the wreck' to be formed into great, evil-smelling structures. Hay was on hand every summer when the council had eventually given in to the inevitable and mowed the savannah, reducing the height of the grass from what seemed like six feet to a more manageable foot or so. No-one ever came back to clear the mowings, so huge amounts of hay would be created by the glorious sun that illuminated all our childhoods, which we would then gather together into towering mounds, just for the hell of it.

I was always a little apprehensive about the Wagon Works. This collection of buildings at the far end of the Wreck always instilled a sense of foreboding. Great clangs and bangs, shouts and oaths, issued from within but I never saw the labourers nor, for that matter, the product of their labours. The Wreck was separated from the Wagon Works by a small brook that ran along that end of the field. Expeditions were sometimes mounted down the steep banks of the brook to try to find anything that had the misfortune to live there. This usually resulted in one or more of us getting very wet and muddy and typically involved an involuntary encounter with a patch of stinging nettles.

Finally, we would head homewards, the ball bouncing rhythmically on the pavement – sorry Cambridge Street! Just past the scrap-yard was a concrete air-raid shelter that none of our group ever offered to investigate, perhaps the memory of its real purpose was still too fresh in the collective mind. Then to Greening's shop on the corner, where the wealthy would dive in to buy chocolate, ice cream, Jubblys or Jungle Juice (frozen three-dimensional triangles of coloured water) and those with only a penny or two to spend would try their luck on the Beech Nut chewing gum machine, knowing that every fourth turn of the handle brought an extra pack and hoping that some fool with more money than sense would have left it just one turn away from that coveted prize!

I went back to the Wreck the other day, consumed by a wave of nostalgia, and found a place of safety play surfaces and basket ball courts, landscaping and trees. The old roundabouts and swings, having wreaked their havoc on the post-war generation, had obviously long since been taken out of service. Of course, it all seems so much smaller now. A walk around the Wreck used to be a daunting proposition; now it's a brief stroll. The scrap-yard has gone, as has the air-raid shelter, and the Beech Nut machine is an ancient memory. The railway lines are still there, much less used and home to diesel fumes rather than steam and smoke. The Wagon Works have given way to a housing estate.

The entrance to the Wreck is quite inviting now, with the greeting 'Welcome' painted in large jolly letters in various languages on the bridge itself, and landscaped grass banks replacing the piles of old cars. The permanent flooding and potholes have gone, as have the toilets. Not unsurprisingly, the stiles providing access to the railway lines have been replaced with high security wire mesh fencing. I wonder if it is still a place of pilgrimage for train-spotters? The brick-built shed of uncertain purpose has gone, to be replaced by a car park. Can you imagine any councillor today trying to sell the idea of the Wreck as it was? 'Well gentlemen, what I think we need is a patch of rough grass set aside for the kiddies. We'll stick it between those two railway lines, just behind the scrap heap. Granted it'll have a bit of heavy industry at one end and we'll have to leave easy access to the lines for the railwaymen but folks should be grateful for what they get, that's what I say.' Probably not.

For all the landscaping and tree planting, the safety surfaces and security fencing, it is still recognizable as the Wreck and I hope it still carves a place in the hearts (if not the foreheads) of today's young as much as it did when an extra pack of Beech Nut was the height of excitement.

Philip R. Whiteland

The Tramways football team, 1904.

Fred's Snippet

I remember we were out playing one morning when we saw some men pushing a yellow aeroplane up to Rolleston Road to try it out. It was made by the Bursted Aviation Co. which was by the side of the canal bridge. On the opposite side of the road was the canal basin and nearby was the soup kitchen. I have fetched many a jug of soup from there.

CHAPTER 3
Aspects of War

Four generations of the Coltman family in the trench named after the hero. (Burton Mail)

Bill's Bit for King and Country

It was a day just like any other except there was a war on and Bill and his brothers were going into town to the Drill Hall in Horninglow Street to enlist in the British Army. It was January 1915. By June Bill was saying goodbye to his wife Eleanor and young son Charles and was on his way to France, not knowing what lay ahead. Bill was born at Tatenhill Common,

Rangemore on 17 November 1892. His father Charles Coltman died when Bill was a very small child leaving his widow, Annie, to support four sons and a daughter by delivering milk with a horse and cart. Bill went to Rangemore School until 1904, when he was twelve. He followed in his father's footsteps as a gardener and worked for Colonel C.J. Goer at Bleak House on Ashby Road and, while tending a garden at Repton, he met Eleanor Dolman, a servant in the house. They married on 8 January 1913. Later that year they had a son Charles and then in 1923 they had a daughter, Dorothy.

Bill was twenty-three when he enlisted in the 216th North Staffordshire Regiment and, in June 1915, went off to France. He did his training at Rouen and joined 'A' Company, 16th Battalion in October. It was after the battle of Gommecourt that Bill felt that the act of killing was contrary to his religious beliefs and volunteered to become a stretcher bearer. The division was briefly shipped out to Egypt in January 1916, then in the spring it was to the Western Front and the opening battle of the Somme. In July 1916 Bill's devotion to his duty in attending the wounded earned him a mention in Dispatches.

In February 1917 Bill rescued a badly wounded officer who had come under fire, shielding him with his own body, and was awarded the Military Medal for his gallantry. In June 1917 Bill, by then a Lance-Corporal, distinguished himself again by going out under fire to tend to the wounded and he was awarded a Bar to his Military Medal.

Only a fortnight later Bill won the Distinguished Conduct Medal for organizing the evacuation of badly wounded men whilst under continuous shell fire and for searching open ground to make sure no wounded had been left behind. He finally returned exhausted.

On 28 September 1918 near Bellinlise, Bill dressed and carried many wounded men under heavy artillery fire without rest. In addition he was a most valuable means of communication bringing back with his wounded accurate information of the advance. In spite of very thick smoke and fog he always found his way about and for this he was awarded a Bar to his Distinguished Conduct Medal. A short time later he went to the assistance of a number of men who were affected by a gas cloud after a British Gas dump was hit. Bill was gassed himself and ended up in a field hospital. Amazingly this was his only wound in the war and he was soon back with his unit on the front line.

During the operations of Manequin Hill, northeast of Sequhart on 3 and 4 October 1918 Bill carried out a heroic act of bravery. Hearing that there were wounded in the front line who had not been attended to, due to the heavy concentrated enemy artillery and machine gun fire, Bill on his own initiative, went forward to find these men. He dressed the wounded and carried each one to his stretcher squad at the back of the line. Saving their lives in that action alone, Bill then dressed and carried wounded men for forty-eight hours without rest. His efforts did not cease until the last wounded man had been attended to. For this he was awarded the Victoria Cross.

Bill's Commanding Officer, Lieutenant-Colonel Ernest Tomlinson, wished to see him one day and sent a runner for him. Bill was attending a casualty in no man's land. When the runner crawled out to him and told him of the Colonel's summons his response was to scowl and say 'you tell the CO to wait, because this chap needs me more'. More than forty years later when the Colonel died at the age of eighty-one, he left Bill £25 in his will.

On a day in May 1919, several months after the end of the First World War, Bill once again said goodbye to his wife and son. This time he knew he was going to return and with his brother George, set out

Bill Coltman. (Photo Reportage Ltd)

for London. When they arrived in the capital they reported to Wellington Barracks and then spent the rest of the day seeing the sights of the city.

He had gone to keep an important appointment, for on the following day he was to receive from King George V the Victoria Cross which he had won for his courage on the battlefields of France for saving, not taking, lives. When the time came for the King to pin the bronze cross with its crimson ribbon to the tunic of the Lance-Corporal, he told him: 'Yours is one of the very few, if not the only case, in the British Army where a man has gained so many distinctions. I heartily congratulate you.' On his return to Burton on Trent, Bill got off the train a stop earlier to avoid a Burton reception committee as he was very modest and a private man.

After the war Bill returned his job as a gardener and later worked for Burton Corporation's Parks Department and was in charge of Winshill's Recreation Ground. During the Second World War Bill responded to his country's call once again and took charge of the Burton Cadets, being commissioned as a Captain.

Bill had Parkinson's disease and it was in the Outwoods Hospital that he died on 29 June 1974. It was fifty-eight years since he won the Victoria Cross for his bravery in saving, not taking, life. Bill was buried with full military honours and gun salute at North Street Meeting Room and then interred in Winshill Churchyard on Thursday 4 July 1974.

On 21 May 1977 the Army paid tribute to Bill by erecting a plaque commemorating his bravery in Burton's Memorial Gardens. Bill's former Commanding Officer said 'his life and example have brought great honour to the regiment and it is most fitting that this permanent memorial should be established here. We have the story of a remarkable man – he had no desire to kill but volunteered to serve his country and became an unarmed stretcher bearer'.

On 29 July 2000 at Whittington Barracks, Staffordshire, a 100-metre trench was opened and named the Coltman trench after Bill. Three generations of Coltmans attended the ceremony complete with military band. It was followed by a re-enactment of an advance over the top by British soldiers.

Mrs J. Coltman

A Country Lad's War

In 1939 I was eight years old and lived in the village of Kings Bromley (which I still do). On Sunday 3 September everyone stayed inside to listen to Prime Minister Neville Chamberlain on the wireless telling the world that a state of war now existed between Britain and Germany. Following this, us kids met in the usual place, under the tree across the road. After debating the issue at length for at least thirty seconds, we decided that we were too young to be sent to the trenches, therefore it would not affect us unduly. This theory was soon shattered because we wandered along to a house down the road where a lady who sold crisps, pop and chocolate from her front door said, 'Make the most of these because we may not get any more as there is now a war on'. The war had only started twenty minutes ago and already our supply of crisps was under threat. We felt that if this was the attitude that Adolf Hitler had adopted he would go to the top of our hate list.

We attended Richard Crosse School at Kings Bromley which attempted to educate the under-elevens. I didn't particularly like school except when I was put in quarantine for two weeks and unable to attend because my sister had measles. My main ambition at this time was to become a 'milk monitor', because school milk arrived in two crates on a Whieldons Green service bus. This meant that the monitors had to go out of the class and wait on the road for the bus, remove the crates of milk and take them into school, ready to be quaffed at playtime.

Overnight in the summer of 1940 the number of pupils receiving education at the school doubled due to the arrival of fifty-two children who had been evacuated from Margate in Kent. They left the Battle of

Britain raging over their home town and quickly accepted the tranquillity of rural Staffordshire. We found their accents very different from our own and there was a great deal of good-natured teasing. They had a 'barth' while we had a 'bath'. Nevertheless we were soon integrated. One boy caught a baby rabbit and put it under the lid of the piano. The teacher froze in fright when as the rabbit moved it appeared that the piano was playing without any visible pianist. She very quickly unfroze and vented her fury on the culprit. After a few months some of the 'vacs' went back to Margate, but others stayed until the end of the war; some still visit Kings Bromley. One little girl never returned to Margate because she disappeared in the floodwaters of the river Trent whilst playing with friends – her body was found in the weir at Alrewas four miles away a week later. She is buried in All Saints' churchyard at Kings Bromley.

The village was cared for medically by doctors Charles and Gerald Armson who were known by their Christian names to avoid confusion. They operated from Yoxall, which boasted a cottage hospital and a wooden lean-to dispensary known as the surgery. When illness struck a family in Kings Bromley, and the doctor was required, the method of getting medical attention was quite unique. As there were few people in the village who owned a telephone, you contacted a lady who lived near the crossroads. She then placed a newspaper held down with a house brick onto a garden wall in Yoxall Road. When the doctor saw the newspaper as he drove through on his daily rounds, he called at the lady's house where he was given directions to find the patient. Simple!

In the very deep snow of January 1940 the village was cut off for about two weeks. Even

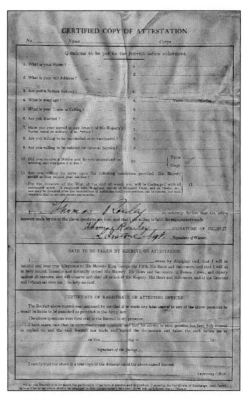

Army form B2505A; Thomas Rowley enlisted for the duration of the First World War. (Mrs M. Wright)

the baker who delivered by horse-drawn van had to leave the bread about two miles outside the village; this had to be collected by men from the village who had dug a path to that point. The doctor could not get through in his car so he visited patients in Kings Bromley on horseback. I was walking through the snow in Alrewas Road when the good doctor rode up. Dismounting, he said to me, 'Now hold my horse, boy, please, while I make a house call'. This horse seemed huge as I stood in the snow, hanging onto the reins. Suddenly, salvation! I saw another lad coming towards me. Thinking quickly, I lied, 'Hey up, youth, the doctor says you've got to look after his horse'. He

I return to the organ, this time keeping my eye on the lead weight. (C. Cooke)

took the reins, and I was free of the snorting beast. This was one of the biggest mistakes of my young life, for at that moment the doctor reappeared, pressed sixpence into the lad's hand, and thanked him for looking after the horse. As he marched off to buy a Mars bar from the shop, his elation was only exceeded by my frustration.

Going to Yoxall surgery at night to collect prescriptions or see the doctor meant going by bus at 6 p.m. and then walking back, since that was the last bus of the night. Unless, of course, you were lucky enough to own a bicycle with dynamo lighting. The surgery was very small so it

meant on busy nights some people had to stand outside in the elements until the queue inside had gone down. On one very congested night the dispenser put her head round the door and requested that anyone whose complaint could be suffered another twenty-four hours go home and return the next day. There were no volunteers so the request was repeated. Suddenly a Kings Bromley man made a dramatic exit, saying loudly as he did so, 'I'm going home to die in bed'. I don't think he did because very few people seem to die of chilblains!

My Dad was an ARP warden, of which there were three in Kings Bromley, and as the village did not boast a siren the wardens had to cycle round the village blowing whistles. Short, sharp blasts warned of an air raid, and long blasts indicated 'all clear'. One night Hitler directed the might of the Luftwaffe against Kings Bromley when ten bombs fell in a line across the western end of the village, blowing the glass out of the greenhouses at a nursery. Also one lone bomb was dropped in a field and a family living near by heard the soil raining down on their roof after the explosion.

On a foggy Saturday night, 17 January 1942, a Wellington bomber from nearby RAF Lichfield was heard flying very low, crossing the village several times. My family thought the pilot was having difficulties locating the airfield in the fog. Suddenly it flew over lower than before, but the engine roar did not die away as previously. It was replaced by a huge explosion and the crackle of ammunition going off which continued late into the night, as did the glow in the sky from the burning aircraft, which had crashed into a wood. Sunday morning dawned with a pall of smoke over the village, which proved to

44

be the funeral pyre of seven Australian airmen. They had travelled 12,000 miles to fight for the mother country but, sadly, their lives ended in a Kings Bromley wood.

In September 1942, we eleven-year-olds left Kings Bromley School and went to various schools in Lichfield and Rugeley. I went to King Edward VI School in Lichfield where there was no alternative but to play rugby. Being a soccer fan, I was very envious of my friend George Myatt who went to Rugeley Grammar School where football was taught.

At the end of the Christmas holidays after my first term there I was playing with a friend across the road at the vicarage. My friend's mother said to me, 'You can have these sandals, because Michael does not use them any more.' I politely replied, 'No thank you, I have a pair of sandals.' She said, 'I think you had better have them; you

will need them.' She then sat me down and explained to me that during the afternoon the house that my family lived in had caught fire and had been partially gutted. I was taken into the house at night and, by torchlight, saw the complete horror of the blackened and charred shell of what had been our home. We slept that night, and for the next few months, at the house of a lady whose two sons were abroad in the Forces. Due to the fact that clothing was rationed I started my second term at Lichfield in my cousin's blazer and trousers and the shoes I was wearing on the day of the fire; but I really needed those sandals.

During the war Sunday evening church services were held in the village hall in the winter months. This was because it was impossible to black the church out sufficiently to allow no light to shine outside. The hymns were accompanied by

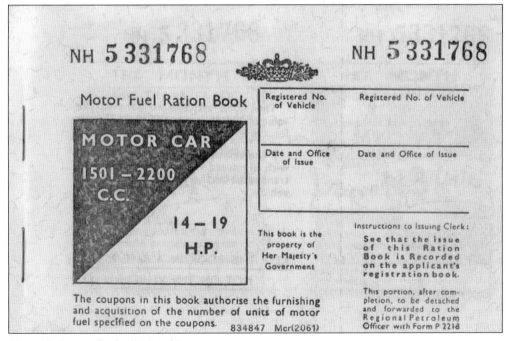

Motor fuel ration book. (F. Smith)

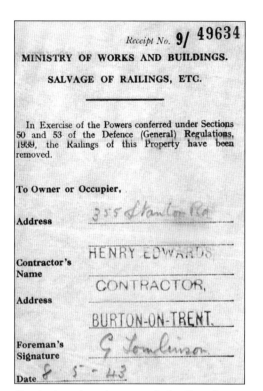

Receipt No. **9/** 49634

MINISTRY OF WORKS AND BUILDINGS.

SALVAGE OF RAILINGS, ETC.

In Exercise of the Powers conferred under Sections 50 and 53 of the Defence (General) Regulations, 1939, the Railings of this Property have been removed.

To Owner or Occupier,

Address   355 Stanton Rd

Contractor's Name   HENRY EDWARDS

Address   CONTRACTOR,

BURTON-ON-TRENT.

Foreman's Signature   G Tomlinson

Date   8 - 5 - 43

Receipt issued on the removal of railings from a private house during the Second World War for the War Effort.

music from the piano. We then went home to listen to Winston Churchill's inspiring speeches on the wireless. Summertime and light nights meant the church was in operation again. Along with an evacuee friend, I went to church to pump the bellows of the organ. The object was to keep a lead weight balanced between two points by gently pumping on a long wooden handle; this kept the correct air pressure in the organ. One night we were in deep conversation, not noticing the lead weight, when suddenly the organ died in the middle of a hymn. To remedy the situation we pumped the handle furiously; the resulting sound being a cross between a stuck pig and a steam train. After the service the vicar and churchwarden, after a summit conference, decided that 'the Cooke boy' was to be banned from the vestry, and that was the last time I pumped the organ. Although the bellows are now pumped electronically, the pump handle and lead weight are still there.

The Home Guard took over the pavilion in the Horticultural Society (show) field and used it for their headquarters. Trenches were dug round it so that it could be protected from attack. Unfortunately, it was alleged that the trenches had been dug too deeply, and Dad's Army could not see over the top, which meant they could only shoot at 45 upwards. This caused us to think that the enemy would all suffer nasty nostril wounds if the allegations were true.

When the war in Europe ended in May 1945, shops, offices, factories and schools closed so that everyone could join in the VE Day celebrations. In Alrewas Road, where we lived, there was a very wide piece of footpath in front of the houses on which a bonfire quickly took shape. Food and drink appeared and a happy crowd watched the lighting. Soon flames were leaping skywards. Unfortunately no one had noticed that the fire had been built beneath some telephone wires which began to melt in the heat and started to drip burning rubber. Frantic men were then seen to be moving the fire along the path with forks, spades, rakes or anything that would not catch fire, until the fire was out of harm's way. Then a biscuit tin full of fireworks saved from before the war was produced and we saw the first fireworks for five years. The next day a village bonfire and fireworks display was arranged at the show field, with more food and drink.

Colin Cooke
Prize Winner

A Birmingham Evacuee

My story unfolds during the 1940s. The date is 14 November and I have just witnessed the destruction of Coventry and its marvellous cathedral. This explosion could be seen from as far away as Cotteridge in Birmingham. These major air raids prompted the government and local authorities to evacuate children of all age ranges from large cities to safety in the countryside, one of the countryside areas being Anslow in Burton on Trent.

Early in 1941 my brother Ron and I left Birmingham New Street laden with two small suitcases and gas masks. We arrived at Burton on Trent railway station very apprehensive, as any two young boys would have been. We were taken by an old coach to Anslow village school where we were billeted out by an appropriate officer. We

were allocated a family – the Heathcotes. They lived at Fish Pond Cottage just outside the village of Anslow, probably about two miles. This was our 'new family' for about fifteen months. We had some very friendly neighbours called the Beddows.

We had to endure a long walk to school each morning or, if we were really lucky, we hitched a lift on the cattle truck. Ron who was older than me had to catch a bus to Tutbury.

Many mishaps happened to us boys as you can imagine. Ron fell through the ice on a nearby lake, I really did think he was gone! I fell in the muck heap in the middle of the farmyard. I was only playing 'tig' with the other children. I had to be hosed down before being sent home minus my Wellingtons which had been lost in the muck!

We had such happy memories of Fish

Anslow Village School. (B. Simkin)

The Firs. (B. Simkin)

Pond Cottage; however, the dry toilet was one I'll never forget. Its contents were tipped on the vegetable patch, no wonder I've never been very fond of eating my greens!

During my first stay, with brother Ron, I used to envy two young girls who were staying across the road from the school. They were evacuees like us. On returning to Anslow in 1943 I was alone. I arrived in Anslow late at night. I knew the two girls had returned home so I was sure there was a space for me at the Firs. I was greeted by Mr Elton who obviously didn't want anymore evacuees. 'No more!' he shouted. 'We had enough of the last two!' Eventually he relented for initially one night. After a good night's sleep he allowed me to stay longer – approximately eighteen months. The Eltons were a wonderful couple who looked after me as their own.

Mr Elton, I think, was of Scottish origin so porridge for breakfast was the order of the day. However, it would have made excellent paving stones! He was also a carpenter and many an hour was passed, by me, admiring his handiwork in his workshed at the bottom of the garden.

I remember vividly the noise from the Army battalion camping in the field behind our house. One morning I awoke early to see them packing up to go to war.

I remember trying to get to school when the snow was waist deep. Many an hour I spent retrieving balls from the garden pond, playing around the Bell Inn and watching Tom at Bill Titterton's farm (Bill is still there today). Tom was taken for a walk one day by a huge black and white bull. One of my favourite pastimes was collecting eggs in the pony trap at Thompstones farm. I also remember helping to put on the tops of the milk bottles and stamping on the dates and consequently getting a lift on the milk tanker as far as Nestlé's Dairy in Uttoxeter. Milk floats from Weston's farm provided me with 'rides' until the horse bolted and I lost that treat!

On one very special occasion I remember being allowed to go to the dance at the Methodist Hall near to the Acorn pub – I'm sure this was my first introduction to Land Army girls. What a wonderful time I was so fortunate to have experienced – local history, Land Army girls, life in a village during the war.

I would finally like to pay tribute to the people of Anslow Village who opened up their homes to evacuees from war-torn towns – Birmingham and Coventry to name but two. They gave us lives in safety and a chance to enable us to grow up and live as normal a life as possible during the wartime years of the 1940s.

Thank you Anslow and your lovely people.

Brian Simkin

I Remember…

I was born in 1936, one of twins, at Anglesey Road, Burton. I believe we lived for a short while on Springfield Road, Swadlincote. My first memories are of 24 Duke Street, Burton.

Dad seemed quite far-seeing at the end of the '30s, perhaps far more than we kids gave him credit for as we got older. For months before food rationing started he had taken a small amount of sugar, tea and other

Titterton Farm. (B. Simkin)

Residents of Duke Street VE Parade fancy dress party outside St Margaret's church, Shobnall Street. (I. Hingley)

dry goods out of the weekly shopping supplies and stored them in large empty milk tins then sealed the tops with sticky tape. All these tins he put on the top shelf of the store cupboard; this was commonly at the side of the living room fireplace. He intended that when rationing started we would have a little extra to make life more bearable when things got scarce. I remember some time later, he came home on leave to find all his carefully stored provisions had quickly gone due to my mother's younger sister's knowledge of this store who had scrounged some commodities for herself. My mother could not bring herself to refuse as my aunt had a daughter the same age as us. Dad went spare and I do remember the row over it.

One evening after dark during the blackout I remember standing at our front door listening to German bombers going overhead. I realise now they were going east from west, perhaps returning to Germany from the Liverpool or Manchester areas. One of our neighbours took their baby son in a clothes basket to the air-raid shelter which was located under Grants of St James in Cross Street (now part of the Bass boiler house).

I remember newspaper ripped into squares in the outside toilet; National margarine; National tea bags and sugar; pickling eggs and one quarter of sweets per month; seeing a group of German prisoners being marched along Hawkins Lane from their work one cold snowy day. There were dray horses everywhere and a council dustcart caught fire in Cross Street due to hot ashes from someone's dustbin. Dustbins were often full of ashes from the fire grates. The dustmen would carry the bins on their shoulders from your back yard out to the streets. I wonder how many of those men suffered from hernias – they earned their Christmas tip in those days. We kept any newspapers that had been used for things such as fish and chip wrapping to assist the lighting of the washing copper in the kitchen; very often this paper had chip cooking fat on it and therefore it ignited well.

There were allotments where the Technical College now stands, and two up, two down cottages in Slater's yard, down an entry off Moor Street, with blue brick paths to each door, earth or ashes covering the bulk of the yard and a toilet block of night spoil pans for each house in the yard. How families managed to be reared in those cold brick-floored cottages has always been a wonder to me. You had peg rugs on the floor, or if you were really well off, coconut matting. Briggs foundry was then in Moor Street, its chimney belching black smoke over the area to settle as soot over the washing lines. The bath was on Friday evenings in front of the fire, with water heated from the copper; kids first, then Mum and Dad after we had gone to bed. It was common in those days to put a clean shirt on a Monday morning for work or school and be expected to wear it all week. We had two bags of coal per two weeks, no toilet soap to speak of and certainly no washing-up liquids, Lux soap powder or Persil having to be used for everything. Enamel washing up bowls were repaired

Officers of RAF Fauld wait on the local people at their Christmas dinner.

with washers.

We played football, cricket, rounders and three stones in the street – no traffic problems then. The goal posts and wickets were chalked onto the wall of what was then Ind Coope's cooperage. The chalk was renewed on the wall so many times the posts and wickets could still be seen on the walls years after we kids had grown up.

The only things we had to watch out for were the once-an-evening patrol of the area policeman and Radford's horse-drawn bread van. Radford's had a bakery in Stanley Street with a shop to the front in Moor Street. Their horse and bread cart delivered local to the town centre. On the last call of the day in Union Street, if the delivery man forgot and slammed the rear door to the dray, the horse knowing this was the last delivery,

bolted down Duke Street heading for home leaving the delivery man to run after him. The horse, then going too fast would turn into Moseley Street and shoot straight across the road into Ind Coope's barrel storage yard sliding to a stop on the cobbles.

I was just about eight years old when Hanbury dump blew up and can remember the school play yard tilting like in an earthquake. My father returned home after four days helping the rescue efforts; he stood on newspaper in the back kitchen and my mother peeled off his overalls that were so thick with mud it looked as if the garment would stand up by itself. His wellington boots were so full of mud my mother had to cut them off his feet.

Ian Hingley

Burton's Reserve Fire Service during the Second World War. At the extreme right on the middle row is Doris Manning; third from the left on the middle row is Muriel Wright. Women worked in the offices during the day and slept three nights a week at Belvedere House on call. This involved going with the firemen to run the mobile canteen. (Mrs M. Wright)

The Prisoner of War Committee, 1939-1945. Standing on the extreme left is Mrs M. Wright. From left to right, front row: Mrs Barman, Mrs E. Thomson Evershed, Alderman John Jones, Mr Tommy Curtis (Chairman of the Burton Co-op who gave his name to Curtis Court in Horninglow Road). The Committee was formed to raise funds for our men captured abroad. This was done by arranging dances at the Town Hall, collecting round the cinemas, raffles etc. They packed parcels for the POWs on a Saturday at the Co-op shoe shop in Byrkley Street. They also arranged teas for POWs' wives and children. (Mrs M. Wright)

Fred's Snippet

The Fauld explosion caused a crack to appear in the spire of Christ Church at the top of Uxbridge Street. The police called at the house opposite and told the family to go to the workhouse to stay because if it toppled it would fall on to their house. They were there for a week. The spire was taken off.

CHAPTER 4
Landmarks

Burton Cemetery Memorial. (B. Cunliffe)

A Burton Boy Made Good

To the right of the main path in Burton cemetery, shaded by a lime tree, stands a towering stone monument finished by a large cross on top. On three sides are inscriptions to the memory of four young children, including twins, who died between 1860 and 1867 all under the age of four years. They were the dearly loved children of John and Elizabeth Wayte. The fourth side, where it would be reasonable to find the parents' names inscribed, remains blank.

John Wayte was born in October 1833 in Burton, the eldest of six children. At seventeen years of age he was working in his father John's grocery and wine merchant business situated at No. 7 High Street, one of several provisions stores owned by the family in Burton town centre. His long day would likely be spent among tea, coffee, sugar, spices, bacon and hams, and not until 8 p.m. weekdays and 11 p.m. Saturdays, would the 'closed' sign appear in the shop doorway. Within walking distance of the shop were the cheesemaker, candle and tallowman, and the oil and colourman who would supply DIY and other household requirements of the mid Victorian household.

John's Uncle Thomas employed and housed several men and servants in his butchery business in Lichfield Street and at the beginning of the century his grandfather, Thomas, had been a felman dealing in cattle and hides. It was a world of prosperity into which John was born and it was expected that he follow his forbears in assuring the continuity of the business.

At the early age of forty-five his father died, leaving him and his mother Anne Maria to continue, and it was during this period that he married a local girl, Elizabeth Smith, and produced the four ill-fated children, the eldest being interred at St Modwen's as the cemetery was yet to open. By way of consolation a surviving child, Thomas Edwin, was born in 1865.

In 1870 John decided that the grocery trade had lost its appeal. Together with Elizabeth and young Thomas Edwin, he joined the tide of emigrants westward to the United States, no doubt to start a new life and put past misfortunes behind them. He was not the first of the family to take this route as his uncles Edwin, William

Elizabeth Wayte. (B. Cunliffe)

and Alfred had made their home in Chicago earlier in the century.

Emigration in those days was not a simple procedure, though this did not deter the many who set their sights on a better life in a new country. By the middle of the nineteenth century some 200,000 a year from the UK and Ireland were leaving Liverpool to face an uncertain future. The scene at Liverpool dock gates on the morning of departure of a ship with a full complement of emigrants was an exciting spectacle. Usually a large number of spectators and relatives turned up to witness the final departure amid laughter and tears for their loved ones, many of whom they would never meet again. Having undergone final inspection and checks, passengers would be allowed to take up their quarters. Boxes and trunks with all their worldly goods went with

John Wayte. (B. Cunliffe)

them, together with a small stock of provisions. Dancing between the decks added to a mood of excited anticipation, and anyone in possession of a fiddle or Irish bagpipes was sure to be popular. But as the hour before departure approached the music ceased. As the ship was towed out, hats were raised, handkerchiefs waved, and long shouts of farewell echoed from the shore, and responded from the ship.

The thoughts of John and Elizabeth as they boarded the vessel, leaving behind close family, can only be imagined. However there was no time for brooding and regrets as John set to work providing for his family on arrival in Chicago. He found employment at Munger's laundry. Early training in business proved most useful when learning the tricks of the trade from Mr Munger, and after twelve months he felt ready to launch out in business on his own account, opening the Home Laundry on State Street, Chicago. The venture proved so successful that Mr Munger sought John's services in jointly managing his own business while away on extended business trips.

About this time a great fire struck Chicago and in common with other branches of business, the laundries were nearly all destroyed. Around 300 Chicago residents perished and 90,000 were made homeless. Fortunately, the Home Laundry escaped the inferno, but it extended to within one block of its premises.

John continued to prosper, moving to larger premises in Dearborn Street, though according to the National Laundry Journal of 1894, this was not his only distinguishing feature. His pocketbook was ever open to alleviate the suffering of the needy, and his laundry was a place of refuge for many homeless people. Piles of soiled linen were converted into 'shakedowns' and provided a place of refuge until permanent homes could be found.

He was ever alert to new technology and was one of the first laundrymen to adopt the revolutionary steam system. But despite the riches his business acumen had brought him, his personal life was dogged by premature bereavement. Two more children born in Chicago did not live to maturity and his wife Elizabeth died in 1880, ten years after their new life began.

While America obviously suited him from a business point of view, when the time was right he came back to his home town on a short visit and found himself a new bride, Caroline Bull, who bore him four children, only two of whom survived infancy.

On a May afternoon in 1894 he left his laundry office at four o'clock where, according to his staff, he had been in particularly happy mood, promising to see them early next morning. After supper he attended a prayer meeting at his beloved Baptist church where he was a deacon and long time member. But after delivering a fervent prayer he became suddenly ill, dying later that night of a heart condition. He was sixty-one, and his youngest son just nineteen months.

The blank side of the memorial in Burton cemetery is no longer a mystery. There lie 3,800 miles of land and ocean between the remains of his four dearly loved Burton children and his burial place at Mount Hope cemetery, Chicago. It would surely be a fitting reward for a successful and kindly gentleman if they were now reunited in spirit.

B. Cunliffe

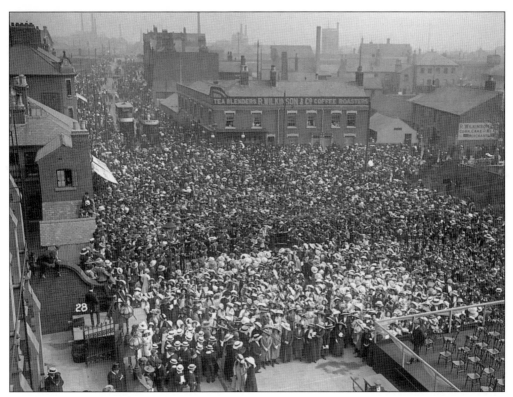

The crowds stream over the Station Bridge and gather in anticipation of the ceremony. (A.T.W. Moody, Acorn Photography)

Michael Arthur Bass

The memorial to Michael Arthur Bass, 1st Baron Burton, stands prominently in King Edward Place. An impressive 24 feet of granite and bronze yet so familiar that few Burtonians take much notice. Of those that do, how many now, less than a century after his death, know why he was honoured with such a grand statue? Most people will of course make the connection with Bass Brewery. He deserves to be remembered for his impact on the town and not reduced to acting as an elaborate traffic island for vehicles circling outside the Town Hall.

Michael Arthur's grandfather, William

Bass, moved to Burton from London to found the family brewery in 1777. It was the year the Trent and Mersey Canal opened with its promise of reliable access for local businesses to wider markets. Within fifty years Bass had grown to dominate the town's thriving brewing industry, continuing to expand throughout the nineteenth century. Under the stewardship of M.T. Bass, Michael Arthur's father, exports of Bass beer played a major part in securing Burton worldwide fame. This successful exploitation of Burton's waters brought jobs, growth and prosperity to the town.

Michael Arthur was born in 1837 and educated at Harrow and Trinity College,

From the speakers' platform Sir Oswald Mosley offers his tribute watched by the Dowager Lady Burton (seated slightly forward on his left). (A.T.W. Moody, Acorn Photography)

Cambridge. At the age of twenty-eight, he followed his father into Parliament representing the local area as a Liberal MP, quickly earning a reputation as a political hard hitter and a champion of ordinary working people. Although his father had steadfastly refused all honours and remained plain Mr M.T. Bass, Michael Arthur accepted a Baronetcy in 1882 and elevation to the House of Lords in 1887. King Edward VII was a close friend and along with most of the leading figures of the day enjoyed Lord Burton's hospitality, either locally at Rangemore Hall or at the Bass's grand house in London's Mayfair.

Lord Burton's gifts to the town embraced sporting trophies and equipment for organizations such as the local Territorial Volunteer force. Michael Arthur's more substantial contributions are architectural and include the Ferry Bridge, Andressey Bridge, the Town Hall's Council Chamber, the former Liberal Club in George Street (now converted to other uses), St Chad's – arguably Burton's finest church – and fittingly King Edward Place itself, where his memorial now stands.

Michael Arthur was clearly good company, and for half a century was the hub around which both the social and commercial life of Burton revolved. News of his death in London in the early evening of 1 February 1909, though not entirely unexpected after declining health, still came as a shock. Special late editions of local papers were rushed out and word quickly spread. Tributes were paid to his 'kind and gracious disposition'.

After more than £3,000 had been raised by local subscription, and on the advice of Birmingham Art Gallery and the Royal Academy, sculptor F.W. Pomeroy was commissioned to produce a statue. Lord Burton is depicted in his peer's robes over the uniform of a honorary colonel in the Staffordshire Volunteers. Bronze panels on the pedestal show the family coat of arms, an emblem of peace and the inscription 'Erected by upwards of 6,000 of his friends and fellow-townsmen in remembrance of one whose life was devoted to the good of others.'

The scenes witnessed at the unveiling of this memorial two years after his death offer an insight into the extent of Lord Burton's popularity. All the shops have closed and at 2 p.m. on an unseasonably hot Saturday, 13 May 1911, a crowd of around 15,000 spectators gathers around King Edward Place. The Town Hall is suitably decorated for the occasion with flags and greenery. Eager for any glimpse of the ceremony the crowd spills out into the surrounding streets, some of the throng clambering onto window ledges and walls in search of vantage points. Inside the special barriers, invited guests and official representatives have a ringside view of the speakers' platform. Bands are playing. Outside the restricted zone, in the heat and jostling crush, Corporation trams are converted into impromptu grandstands for the duration. The Bishop of Lichfield offers prayers and there are speeches by Sir Oswald Mosley and the Mayor before the Earl of

All eyes are on the stage as the Earl of Dartmouth unveils the memorial. (A.T.W. Moody, Acorn Photography)

Dartmouth, Lord Lieutenant of Staffordshire, carries out the official unveiling. Harriet, Dowager Lady Burton, watches accompanied by her sisters and only child, Nellie, the new Lady Burton. Official proceedings over, the dignitaries retire to enjoy the buffet waiting for them in the Town Hall and the assembly begins to disperse. All have played their part in a brief moment of Burton's history.

Michael Arthur Bass promoted the prosperity of the town and the results are still with us today. As a man of personal integrity, Michael Arthur Bass well deserved his more direct memorial.

Richard Stone

Jubilee Hall. (P. Molloy)

Jubilee Hall

There it sits, almost alone, like an intact survivor from a Hiroshima of devastation and redevelopment. It occupies a corner: a crossroads in more ways than one. On one side of the right angle it ends and there is just space; along the other the road, New Street, it continues in a line of Victorian buildings until it, too, peters out into modernity in the shape of a new precinct. One day it will perhaps be an island wondering how it got there at all unmoored from its once familiar surroundings. The old meets the new along the same street plan, a blend of the best of the past and the possibilities of the future. On the outside is a date-stone and a name: Shaftesbury House, and the date '1893' scrolled decoratively onto the wall.

A 'Technics' sign, unapologetic in affirming the twenty-first century, sticks out from the wall on Orchard Street; and from the photographer's viewpoint is perfectly in line with the confident calligraphy of 1893 – the contrast makes him smile. A meeting with the two sign makers would yield some interesting discussion.

I remember it from my childhood in the sixties, with a Wembley arena-like relish, the Jubilee Hall, or the plain old 'Jube' for short. A hall at the back of the building that seemed immense when in fact it was quite modest in size; but then childhood is such a miniaturized world, polished wooden dance floor, cosy bars and taprooms still with a flavour of wartime. I remember velvet-covered, studded fold-up wooden seats. Everything about it was familiar, warm and personal: spilled ale, sodden beer mats, overflowing ashtrays and the happy haze of cigarette smoke. Our parents took my cousin and me when we were children and right through our adolescence. When we were younger we grabbed our bottles of pop and played about the building only returning at evening's end, when we needed a refill or when our parents sought us out for some reason, elusive in roaming its corridors and snug bars, watching our parents from a distance. It was a small world, which seemed immense, whose nooks and crannies we would inhabit and explored during those evenings, studying the adults, watching their behaviour. Our mothers on their trips to powder their noses would pet us if we were about the doorways, and we relished the attention of our fathers when we came back to our table. Finding the spaces where we could be ourselves, the noise and the music and the laughter and the pure life of it – those evenings still seem fresh in the memory.

Hitting the heady years of teenagedom, we strayed further afield down Union Street, perhaps with some money to buy chips, asserting our independence, bigger, wondering about the future and our place in it. The Jubilee was now less of a playpen and began to assume the role of venue; a place to be, not a place to play

It was already a dinosaur the last time I paid a visit in the late seventies. I have a recollection of stopping by with a friend, John Raynor, both of us aged about sixteen or seventeen, locking up our pushbikes outside and going in to see our dads who were having a beer and a game of cribbage. It never meant much to me at the time that a culture was passing by, after all how could I know? It wasn't a

fashionable haunt, and not one I frequented, when my pubbing days began while at the Technical College down the road. Then I was chasing a good time and that didn't include supping ale in old working men's bars. I never saw it, though, as living on borrowed time. It was a museum piece to my youth, immemorial and imperishable, a repository of some boyhood memories. Sometime in the early to mid-eighties it was disembowelled, the patina of history ripped out and thrown into a skip, dust to dust, ninety years or so of residual memories swept away as easily as that. What use would an eighteen-year-old of the time have for such memories that weren't their own, in the chrome and glitz nightclub it had now become? My sense of disappointment on entering the building in its new guise was profound: the place was unrecognizable, a noisy, flashing beery paean to disco, the eighties and progress. It was me, discovering the meaning of nostalgia about the same time, who noticed its absence and felt its loss. I wanted it to be the same place I had walked into with my friend that time, when I didn't care a hoot if it were demolished the next day. Now when I visit my home town I peer up at the name and date-stone with a protective air, thankful that it has been saved from the planners' extermination programme; much of the area, once homogeneous, has gone, and one wonders how long it too will be spared – as long as it functions as an entertainment venue perhaps.

To me it is forever enshrined in my memory. In a town where so much has been erased, it's good that some things remain. Burton was a Victorian town built around the brewing industry, created

Burton market Hall, erected in 1882. Most of us will still remember this tree which has only recently been replaced. (B. Hudson)

largely in the second half of the nineteenth century and remaining more or less extant until the sixties and the first wave of improvements that swept the country. The old buildings, many of them sub-standard, were swept away in the zeal for redevelopment. Much of it was right but much, also, unnecessary. I suppose the era of the sixties and seventies was one of deletion; the worst of the past had served its purpose and was redundant. I lived through it with the Victorian as the template, the psychic street map. The Jubilee Hall was a product of a past era, birthed in the late Victorian era, a place for the working classes, a concept, a generation and a set of values that trickled through to the late seventies and, dying, was finally and ironically swept away by that arch-Victorian herself, Margaret Thatcher – a strange revolutionary role. Now the Jubilee hangs on while all around it alters. It is a product of its time, facelifted on the inside, like a reformed soul, but the external kept pristine and innocent while what is not visible from the outside is made ugly.

I hope it remains as a cherished memory, so that in passing I can recall a bygone age, however brief my association, and however ailing and moribund it was at the time.

Phil Molloy

King John on his first visit to Burton from 3 March to 1 April 1200 confirmed a Charter for a market to be held on Thursdays of each week. The King also granted permission for a fair of three days' duration to be held commencing on the eve of St Modwen, which is 29 October. This Charter was confirmed by Henry III on 12 August 1227 and again by Edward IV in 1468. (B. Hudson)

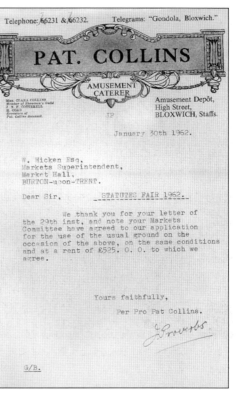

The market hall was improved and modernized in 1938 at no cost to the ratepayers, although the scheme itself cost approximately £6,000. (B. Hudson)

Fred's Snippet

When they pulled down the church in Horninglow Street they believed there was gold placed under the foundation stone but they didn't find it. They then realised there was a foundation stone the other end of the church as there had been a previous church on the same site. It was too late, all the rubble had been taken to the building site near the station and the new roundabout is over it.

Tales of the Square

The late Harry Curtis, one-time lecturer at the Burton Technical College, knew a great deal of the history of Burton. His advice to me, a new recruit teaching history, was 'Take them out and about and let them find out.' I did just that and the pupils found it very rewarding.

One such discovery was Dame Paulet's Almshouses, situated in Bank Square opposite the Market Place. At that time – 1974 – the building was used by the Corporation's Weights and Measures Department. I told the pupils that the building was due to be demolished to make way for the new shopping precinct.

Now you may ask, as the pupils did, who was Dame Paulet and why did she build the Almshouses? That was in 1598 and they were built to house six women of the town who were old and had no means of support. Dame Paulet was Elizabeth, the daughter of Walter Blount, sister to John Blount who was a landowner in Burton and played an important part in the affairs of Burton.

The pupils of the newly-built Horninglow Secondary School were disgusted to learn that a piece of Burton's history was about to be demolished to make way for another shopping precinct. Something had to be done.

They proposed that the Almshouses should remain for their historic value and then wrote to 'Burtonian' of the Burton *Daily Mail* – a champion for sure. They drew up a petition to be signed by those people who also did not want the building pulled down. Burtonian gave us a column in the Burton Mail and a lot of help.

Lady Gothard, wife of Sir Clifford Gothard, joined the crusade and came to school to sign the petition. She told the Burton Mail that there was so little of old Burton left that she wanted to try and save this little piece of history.

The pupils carried on their work of collecting signatures – more than 1,000 in the following weeks. Christopher Johnson, Norman Parker, Pamela Bailey, Josephine Curtis and many younger pupils played a big part in collecting and delivering the signatures. Students from the Burton Technical College also played a part with the petitions. The Town Clerk, Mr Henry Meades, remarked, 'The enthusiasm and energy shown by the pupils must be welcomed.' The young champions knew that they could not convince the council but some good came of the crusade. Fifth-former Christopher Johnson received a letter from them to say that, although the building could not be saved in its entirety, the council promised that the doorway of the building would be saved and placed in one of the walls of the new Littlewoods building which was to be erected on the site. It was also suggested at the council meeting that members of the council should go and

Mrs Harvey with Horninglow pupils, 1974. (E.L. Harvey)

visit the almshouses.

As the building progressed the crusaders kept watch on what was happening. When D Day dawned there were some misgivings. Burtonian phoned the planning development office and spoke to the Planning Officer, Mr Makin, asking if the doorway would be positioned in the new structure as promised. Because of its delicate nature it had to be put in last. They kept their promise.

When the day came and the doorway was in situ, I was invited to go and watch the proceedings. I felt proud of the crusaders. I wonder if they can remember the mammoth task they took on. Harry Curtis would have been happy and I think his daughter, Josephine, was proud to be part of it.

In 1966 the Laing Development Company asked schools to select names for the new Central Area. Horninglow pupils named St Modwen's Walk, Fennel Walk, Swan Walk and Paulet Square. Alderman J.W. Parker once said 'The younger generation of the town would be living with the names chosen maybe longer than the councillors. Not quite so. In 1994 the second battle of Paulet Square took place, when it was re-named Cooper Square, the new home of the Burton Cooper.

Mrs E.M. Harvey

CHAPTER 5
Schooldays and Working Days

The Technical High School badge with Finneys Post embroidered in gold. (D. Bladon)

Burton Technical High School

The Hadlow and Spens Reports were both incorporated into the 1944 Education Act. This Act created 146 Local Education Authorities throughout England and Wales. There would be three stages of free education – Primary, Secondary and Further. Religious education lessons would be compulsory, and the school leaving age would be raised to fifteen.

The Act advocated 'parity of esteem'

between children, regardless of the schools they attended. Burton, though small, nevertheless was a C ounty Borough and a forerunner in many fields, not least education, and early in 1946, the Education Committee decided to put the 1944 Act into operation.

However, no sooner had the Education Committee set things in motion, than a spanner was thrown into the works, for on 16 June 1946, the Labour Government sent out a circular to all LEAs advocating the introduction of comprehensive education, defined as 'secondary education of all children in a given area without organization on three sides'. As a result, the first comprehensives came into existence; in London, Essex and parts of Wales. Here in Burton, the circular was either not received, or if it was, it was just ignored, for the Burton Technical High School opened for business on schedule on 3 September 1946, and for the next nineteen years, it was to be a significant and unforgettable part of the town's post-war history.

First and foremost, there were clearly going to be accommodation problems. The premises selected for the Tech's HQ was the former Broadway Central School on Branston Road, a school designed to accommodate 360 children, and with the first intake of 576, fun and games were about to begin.

Why choose Branston Road? Because of its more adequate facilities! The two Central Schools in Guild Street were closed in 1941, and were used as billets for wounded soldiers who were coming home from the war. All the other schools were grossly overcrowded. What happened to the kids of Broadway Central School? They were simply upgraded. In the five years from 1941 to 1946, Broadway Central's name was changed three times, from Broadway Central, then it became the Intermediate School, finally becoming Burton Technical High School in September 1946.

That did not solve the problem of over 200 surplus kids. This was to rise to 500 in later years, when the school had 813 pupils on its books. This was in 1960. The year before, the total came to 810. After these two peaks, the intake gradually decreased until, in the school's final year (1964/65), the total dropped to just over 300.

To accommodate the children, various premises were commandeered. Whilst Branston Road was to be the main building, other buildings were used for various subjects. All Saints' Church Hall for PT (Physical Torture!), Clarence Street Chapel for English, Wellington Street For domestic science, Anderstaff Lane Infants' School for maths, Union Street for commerce and engineering and, later in 1948, to everyones's relief, St Paul's Institute entered the equation. We even used the old wartime Nissen huts at St Paul's and at Clarence Street! They talk about split sites today. These are nothing compared with what we had to endure. Even Burton Corporation's swimming baths on Burton Bridge did nor escape the Tech's clutches!

Mr Smalley once recalled to me that one of his first tasks on joining the school was to stand in for a colleague for a period of maths. The classroom was the Queen Street Methodist chapel. He quite clearly did not know where it was, and when finding it, he really did not believe that he had to teach there. 'But I walked in, the class accepted the situation as normal, and we all got on with the business of maths – the pupils were magnificent and at that point I realized that I was involved in something unique,' said Gordon.

What attracts children most are colours. The school uniform stood out. It was dark brown with gold braiding. The school badge was Finney's Post embossed in gold on blazers, caps and berets. These striking colours stood out against the drab dark blue of the Grammar School and the Girls' High School. We looked very conspicuous as we wended our way to our various destinations for our lessons. How Eric Armstead devised the week's timetable, which went like clockwork, in theory at least, I shall never know.

Many of the teachers are still with us, and some who taught at the Tech went on to teach at Dovecliff Grammar, Wulfric Comprehensive, and in two other cases, Mr Heather and Mr Hartshorn went on to teach at De Ferrers High. Other teachers included Mr Don Sherwin, Ken Neal, Nancy Jones, and the unforgettable F. (Freddie) Baker and P.C.H. (Percy) Davies. Unlike other schools, our desks were mobile! We kept our books at home, and carried them around with us in our satchels. We became as skilful in selecting our textbooks each day, as Mr Armstead had become in devising the school timetable. If we had a sporting fixture, we had to carry our kit as well. It became a way of life for us and, looking back, it obviously did us no harm. I fondly remember the shops we used to pop into as we literally ran from lesson to lesson. Mrs Parson's sweetshop opposite New Street bus park, was one remembered with affection.

Anderstaff Lane Infants' School in Wetmore Road was adapted for children aged five to eleven. There were extremely cramped, little low desks, and even worse chairs, even for us grown-ups – we were twelve. St Paul's Institute was a two-storey building with a very large hall on the ground floor. It was dark, dingy and, although it was not comfortable, it was the best of the three described – albeit not a school building! We went to various chapels, not to worship, but to learn. We would sit in the pews, still wearing our coats, headgear, scarves and, in some cases, gloves. How we managed to write with gloves on, I cannot say, but we did.

My own first personal recollection of the Technical High School was when I learned that I had passed the eleven-plus exam. Wow! I suppose it was mainly due to the fact that I was very happy at Horninglow Junior School under Miss Coward, Mrs Sudale, and Miss Topliss. When I started at the 'Tech', I would catch a Corporation No. 6 bus from Calais Road post office and arrive at Branston Road just in time for assembly. The No. 6 went down Uxbridge Street, and I would dash down All Saints' Road, into South Broadway Street, through the back gate and into school.

The worst day of the week obviously was Monday. Form 1.3, the class to which I had been allocated in September 1947, had five periods of maths down at Anderstaff Lane with Eric Armstead and Gordon Smalley. It was dreadful. One Monday morning, I decided to 'give maths a miss'.

My excuse would be that I had forgotten my books, and as a result, missed the bus. We were scheduled at Branston Road in the afternoon and so I could catch the bus down there at lunchtime, I spent the morning hiding in Horninglow churchyard. I regretted it however, because I was hauled up in front of the Headmaster, Dr Evans, to give an account of myself. Unfortunately for me, Dr Evans had rung my father's employers and reported me missing and he came home as a result. I got home that evening, and got quite a hiding. I decided there and then, maths or no maths, it was better than a good pasting!

Things improved when St Paul's Institute became available in 1948. Wetmore Road School was handed back, and the timetable was adjusted accordingly. Things didn't seem too bad after that. However, I got into trouble once again. There was a low wall around the building, and as boys will be boys, instead of walking sedately through the gateway provided, we would vault the wall. However, some 'snitcher' reported me, and I was hauled up on to the stage and given six of the best.

These two incidents apart, my time at the Tech was a happy one. I was good at drawing, and I often had drawings displayed around the hall at Branston Road. I remember going back some years after I had left, and there were a couple of my drawings still hanging on the wall. A former Desert Rat, Mr Jack Livesey, the art teacher, encouraged me and gave me unlimited amounts of paper so that I could draw for him at home.

We were doing cross-country one afternoon. We changed in the pavilion on Truman's brewery sports ground (now part of Shobnall Fields), and we went over

The 23rd (Burton Tech) Scout group. (D. Bladon)

Sinai, down into Tatenhill Lane, and back along the canal towpath to Shobnall. This particular afternoon, I cut my leg rather badly on some brambles (I still have the scar!) on Sinai, and I was way behind the others. I was walking back along the towpath, my leg still bleeding, when Frank Wilson, the typing teacher, came along on his bike. He gave me a lift on his crossbar to the changing room. Percy Davies was not amused.

If the mornings were mobile, the afternoons were often frantic, through the seemingly endless crossing gates, we would perhaps move to St Paul's for a single period of maths with Eric Armstead, or geography with Nancy Jones, or even join the clattering of typewriters to music (nearly always Strauss waltzes!) with the ever fun-loving Frank Wilson. This could be

followed by a trek over Sinai, or playing football or cricket at Shobnall.

Perhaps, one day, we would assemble at Burton baths, where the thunderous voice of Percy Davies would echo around the ancient building, followed by a quick sprint back to Branston Road, hair wet, socks down, tie askew for a double period of physics and chemistry with Ken Neal, art with Jack Livesey, or French with Don Sherwin. Another venue was the art school in Waterloo Street, where we would have woodwork with Mr Hobby.

There were four houses at the Tech, Cobden (blue), Faraday (red), Shakespeare (yellow), and Wren (green). I was allocated to Wren House. During my five years at the school, I amassed a total of one house point! To this day, I do not know how I achieved this. I shall never know for what I

The 23rd Burton Scouts at camp in Torquay. (D. Bladon)

was given a single house point for. Nevertheless, I broke my duck.

All of this reflected what the Burton Technical High School had come to represent, a hard working, hard playing establishment: it had an enthusiastic group of teachers, almost all of whom had been on military or war service, who were now giving to the children of the town an education which was preparing them for a career as apprentices and trainees in local industry and commerce.

Two such figures who have made the grade, and who came from humble beginnings, spring to mind. One started his working life as an apprenticed plumber, to go on and make a fortune in the building trade generally, and the other has devoted her life to politics. They are, of course, Sir Stan Clarke CBE, and Dame Rachel Dyche DBE.

These two are examples of many success stories, which speak volumes for the school. I left the Tech in 1952 after five happy, hectic years, but it was to go on for another thirteen years. The only other change after my time was the handing back of St Paul's Institute, and moving into Bond Street School, when the Boys' Grammar School moved into their new premises at Winshill in 1957.

The Autumn Term of 1964 witnessed the Tech's final nomadic year. For nineteen years, hundreds of brown and gold clad kids had wandered along Burton's streets to their various destinations. Now all that was about to change, never the likes of which to be seen again.

The Tech achieved grammar school status, and for this, it was to be rewarded with its own purpose-built, state-of-the-art school on the Horninglow/Stretton boundary. It was renamed Dovecliff Grammar School. The uniform remained the same however, and it was not until 1975 that the old brown and gold, which was adopted nearly thirty years previously, was finally replaced with the green of Wulfric Comprehensive. Today, the school still excels. Built on shaky foundations, it is a continuing success story known as the De Ferrers High School.

Back in 1946, with the Corporation Education Committee's blessing, Mr Arthur Blake, Director of Education for Burton, was given his head, and Burton Technical High School, one of only 214 in the country, was founded. Despite the appalling conditions we had to work under, we rose to the challenge, and the success of the school in achieving Grammar School status is now a legendary part of Burton's post-war history.

Dennis Bladon

Fred's Snippet

When I was at school – Horninglow Mixed – four of us boys passed the exam to go to the Grammar School. George Starbuck, Dick Hufton, Alsbrook (I forget his Christian name) and myself. My parents couldn't let me go but the other three all became headmasters.

The School at Walton on Trent

Before education became compulsory in the 1870s almost all that was provided in villages was on a charitable basis through the influence of churches and local benefactors. This was certainly true of Walton on Trent.

Research indicates that the first mention of education in records relating to Walton comes from the will of William Bedford,

Form C1 in 1949. On the extreme left is Dennis Bladon. (D. Bladon)

The class of 1920 at St Peter's School, Stapenhill. On the back row on the left are Muriel and Kenneth Rowley. (M. Wright)

rector of the parish. This is dated 1662 and leaves the sum of £20 to purchase the lease of a close, the rent of which was to be spent on the teaching of three male children of the village to knit stockings and, after they became competent at this, to be taught to read. So knowledge of a trade came before literacy! Bedford's widow, Bridget, reiterated this in 1671 in the form of a deed and added £5 to the bequest.

We do not know where this basic teaching took place. It was probably in the church itself and may also have soon been accompanied by classes inspired by the Sunday School Movement led by Robert Raikes.

There is no direct evidence for the existence of a school. Until a new school was built in the 1980s, the village school had always been on the same site. What is certain and recorded is that in 1760 a Mrs Levett and a Mrs Bailey paid £260 to purchase a close in the nearby village of Linton, the rent thereof to be used to pay a teacher of poor children of the parish whose parents could not afford to pay charges themselves. This suggests the previous existence of a school where charges were indeed made. The school was in the hands of trustees who could decide how long pupils could remain in the school free of charge.

Mrs Levett and Mrs Bailey at the same time (1760) gave a dwelling house for the schoolmaster, a schoolroom and a small plot of land for a playground, again in the hands of the trustees. The Charity Commissioners also reported that in 1825 thorough repairs were carried out to the premises. The same report indicates that each child paid 1d per week with 3d for any additional instruction and poor children being free. By the beginning of the nineteenth century, therefore, Walton had a school, a schoolteacher and a charitable trust for support. It had been created by the influence of the church – the rector was always Chairman of the Trustees – and local philanthropists.

The school logbook records the dimensions of this old school. It consisted of a principal room 20ft by 14ft by 9ft for thirty-two children and a classroom for thirty-eight children of 28ft by 12ft by 8ft. The overcrowding can be imagined. By 1878 this building was seen to be inadequate and it was pulled down. That presented a problem as the logbook entry for 21 June 1878 records: 'Obliged to close school today on account of the school building being taken down in order to build new school, and the barn in which we are to hold the school not being ready for us.' The school reopened in the barn on 8 July and all was well until cold weather arrived. The barn was eventually so cold that parents refused to send their children any longer and its use was discontinued on 28 November. The children of the village had a holiday of over four months until the new school was ready for use on 15 April 1879. Its dimensions are recorded as a principal room of 37ft by 16ft by 19ft and a classroom of 20ft by 16ft by 19ft. This building still stands but is now a private house, having been replaced in the 1980s by a modern building.

What did pupils at the school study and what other activities were there for them? Evidence for the time before the logbook commences (1876) has not been found but we know from other sources the kind of studies that would have been likely. At first there would have been a strong emphasis on reading, writing, numbers and Bible study. Even the reading and writing would have been based on Scripture by the use of battledores – handheld pieces of board with skin stretched across.

The school was an Anglican church school and remains so today. In its early days the influence of the Church and the rector was very strong indeed. There were Bible study and prayers each day, often taken by the rector himself as a frequent visitor. The children often went to church for special services such as Lent and Ascension Day and there were holidays for Sunday school and choir outings. Singing, geography and needlework for girls were early introductions but further changes were limited by the system of 'payment by results'. A school's grant was assessed by the performance of pupils in passing tests in basic subjects set by inspectors and this caused anxious teachers to concentrate on these rather than making attempts to broaden the curriculum.

Under what was known as the Revised Code pupils were divided into separate standards and expected to reach certain levels. The inspectors would test and then report. This system persisted with minor changes until the 1890s and, although it was very narrow, it did establish something approaching a national curriculum. Church schools were also subject to inspection by officials from the Diocese with regard to the teaching of Bible studies and this practice continues today.

From 1903 the school came under the control of the Derbyshire Education Authority and thus directly subject to government influence. Largely because of this there were developments in its curriculum. History and 'drill' (a basic form of PE) soon found places and then

SYLLABUS (REVISED CODE OF 1862)	
Standard I	
Reading	Narrative in monosyllables.
Writing	Form on blackboard or slate, from dictation, letters, capital and small, manuscript.
Arithmetic	Form on blackboard or slate, from dictation, figures up to 20. Name at sight figures up to 20. Add and subtract figures up to 10, orally, from examples on blackboard.
Standard II	
Reading	One of the narratives next in order after monosyllables in an elementary reading-book used in the school.
Writing	Copy in manuscript character a line of print.
Arithmetic	A sum in simple addition or subtraction and the multiplication table.
Standard III	
Reading	A short paragraph from an elementary reading-book used in the school.
Writing	A sentence from the same paragraph slowly read once and then dictated in single words.
Arithmetic	A sum in any simple rule as far as short division (inclusive).
Standard IV	
Reading	A short paragraph from a more advanced reading-book used in the school.
Writing	A sentence slowly dictated once by a few words at a time, from the same book but not from the paragraph read.
Arithmetic	A sum in compound rules (money).
Standard V	
Reading	A few lines of poetry from a reading-book used in the first class of the school.
Writing	A sentence slowly dictated once by a few words at a time, from a reading-book used in the first class of the school.
Arithmetic	A sum in compound rules (common weights and measures).
Standard VI	
Reading	A short ordinary paragraph in a newspaper or other modern narrative.
Writing	Another short ordinary paragraph in a newspaper or other modern narrative, slowly dictated once by a few words at a time.
Arithmetic	A sum in Practice or bills of parcels.

The syllabus from the Revised Code of 1862.

handicraft (1912), home management, hygiene and agriculture (1915), science (1920), gardening (1924), dancing (1925), nature study (1926) and eventually swimming at nearby Burton in 1940. Bible studies and church influence were always a strong presence and oral testimony from older villagers confirms that almost all children in the village were attenders at the Sunday school.

There were other innovations. In 1927 there was the first visit to a cinema – to see *Ben Hur* – and in 1928 to a theatre to see *The Merchant of Venice*. The first occasion of a radio broadcast being used in the school was in 1930 when pupils listened to the service from the Cenotaph on 11 November. By the outbreak of the Second World War the basics of a modern school curriculum were in place and as early as 1934 an inspector was able to report, 'This is a good school with excellent tone.' Pupils took part in village activities such as concerts, garden parties and the traditional crowning of the village May Queen.

There was little variation in the size of the population of Walton between 1800 and 1900 – usually it was around 400. Before school attendance became compulsory in 1870 it would have been voluntary. Walton was always an agricultural community and children would legitimately have been kept away at harvest and other busy times. Some would not have attended school at all though the parish registers do not indicate a high rate of illiteracy. When the logbook commences in 1876 there is concrete evidence.

In 1887 there were 133 pupils on roll and the average attendance was 109. By 1910 there were only 70 on roll and by 1922 only 54 and thereafter the numbers fluctuate between 55 and 90. Conditions must have been very cramped and the equipment poor. The logbook is a mine of information. There are frequent references to poor attendance because of outbreaks of measles, mumps and even scarlet fever, and in the winter the school was often seriously affected by severe weather conditions with children unable to reach school because of heavy snow and flooding. There was also frequent disruption and illegal absence at busy periods such as summer harvest and potato-picking time. There are frequent references to local and national events such as Coronations and war triumphs – most of which merited a holiday.

In 1881 the Census tells us that there were

104 children in Walton between the ages of four and thirteen. The school leaving age was ten. In 1893 it was raised to eleven and to twelve in 1899. By 1918 it had become fourteen. In 1944 came the Butler Act which was a watershed in the history of schools. It meant the end of village and town schools which had catered for the children of most families until they were old enough to go out to work. After its implementation, at the age of eleven children transferred to secondary schools, although a few had won scholarships to local grammar schools for some years beforehand. The character of Walton school had changed for good. It was now a Church of England primary school for pupils up to the age of eleven. Older pupils then transferred from the village to the secondary school at nearby Barton under Needwood as they still do today.

The head of a village school was always a person of some importance in a village community. In early times before the spread of general education he or she would have been one of the few villagers able to read and write fluently and having some knowledge of the outside world. Directories classed head teachers with local landowners, though obviously somewhat lower in the pecking order. However, the early heads of Walton School would not have been trained or qualified. The only criterion was approval by the Church and trustees. Their morals had to be beyond reproach and they had to be staunch supporters of the local church. It was not until after 1870 that trained teachers began to appear in any numbers.

As the number of pupils increased and the demand for education grew there was a shortage of teachers. An inadequate solution was to appoint monitors – older children who would help by teaching younger ones. In 1847 a system of paid pupil teachers was introduced. They had to be at least thirteen years of age and by passing examinations could eventually become qualified. Many served in Walton and the last to be appointed was in 1921. The logbook makes it clear that there were never enough teachers to run the school efficiently and often the entire school was in the charge of one person.

Heads often stayed in a village school for most of their careers and a good example is David Williams who ran Walton school from 1881 until 1923. It is evident from the logbook and the minutes of the parish council, of which he was clerk, and the fact that he was Overseer of the Poor, that he was a pillar of the establishment of the village and the church. His daughter succeeded him as head in 1924. She began her career as a paid monitor in 1897, probably at the age of thirteen, and then became a pupil teacher, eventually leaving Walton for training and qualification.

Another example was Ethel Hine whose father was a joiner in Walton – becoming a teacher was a way for village youngsters to climb the social ladder. She began as a monitor at Walton school in 1903, then became a pupil teacher and eventually an assistant mistress. She returned to Walton as head in 1931 where, as Mrs Hurdley, she remained until 1953. She is buried in the village churchyard.

Neil Adams

From School to Work

I went to school at Clarence Street, the second year after it was built. I used to miss English lessons because the school had this projector which the teachers didn't know

David Williams with pupils in the 1920s at the crowning of the May Queen. (N. Adams)

how to use. They knew I was interested in projectors so they would fetch me out of class to run the film for them. It was a 16mm. My favourite film was *The Scarlet Pimpernel*, the one about the French Revolution. It was black and white of course. Leslie Howard was the actor. I got the bug for films.

I was coming back from the Ox Hay one night past the Electric Cinema and the doorman was stood outside. I was ready to leave school, being thirteen. I asked him for a job. He said to come back with me mother and father and see the manager. I went all dolled up in me best clothes. Mr Arthur Rice was the manager then. He asked me why I wanted to work there. I told him I'd been doing it at school. He gave me a job and I started as a re-wind lad and scrubbing the floors in the projectionist box. There were five of us lads in a small place. I remember when *How Green Is My Valley* was showing, the queue went down to the pavement in High Street, up to the market

and round into Friars Walk. It was always packed and they would queue even in the pouring rain. There was a children's matinée every Saturday and we opened on a Sunday. There were two shows on a Sunday – 4 to 6 p.m. and 6 to 8 p.m. We stayed open during the war until 4 p.m. I had to take the films out of the tins and put them onto spools. We showed a feature film and a short film. The short ones were something like British horse racing and things like that. When it was really packed out I had to take a torch and help the usherette.

The years went on and I joined the Forces. The RAF at Padgate, I went to. There was a big cinema on the camp and it was shut. I told them I was a projectionist and asked if I could open it up, but they wouldn't let me. In 1947 they sent me off with the others to Dover and then on to Calais and on to North Italy, the Desert Airforce. Flight Lieutenant Neville was the chap's name at Welfare and he showed me the film library and asked if I could run it. I was given the key and when I went in it was a right mess. The films needed sorting so I got stuck in and put them in order and gave each a number. I saw all the projectionists from each camp and set up training for them and gave them a certificate. You had to know what you were doing to save the films getting damaged. I remember the Americans liked our films like Blithe Spirit and those sort. The Americans had colour films so we would swap with them. I would take the train with the films and go round the camps dropping and picking up films and on to the next camp where I'd drop off the films I'd picked up from the camp before. I went once a month. The train would go slow through the mountains, youngsters would jump on to the steps outside the carriages and pilfer. I locked myself in down to Naples. I'd go on to Rome, Rimini, Bologna and back through Austria and Vienna, leaving films. The cinemas were mobile with their own generators. Border Guards would wave me through. Never asked for identification. They all knew me, see, because I went every month. In the gardens at Veldon they would play British films till 8 p.m. and then Austrian after that.

After two years in the RAF I came back to the High Street Electric Theatre, but it was all new people and I didn't like it much. I went to the brewery. I taught cellar management by showing films all round the country. The films showed how to manage pubs. Things like: if the toilets were spotless the people would stay but if not then they would go straight out. I went from Stoke to Devon. I was taking my own film by then, 16mm. I took films of the bottling stores but I think it's lost now. I took the Staffordshire Balls at the Town Hall, all the dignitaries and bosses and that. I would show them at

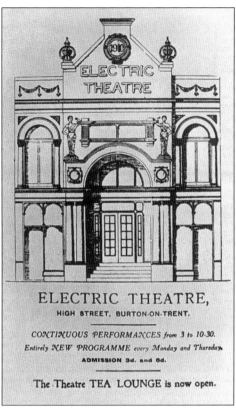

Poster advertising the Electric Theatre, High Street, c. 1940.

the Ind Coope Club in Mona Road. We'd have a film show once a month. I'd show all the new films of the day.

I finished at the brewery after a few years. I borrowed a camera from the brewery to film the Coronation. I went on to Parkers where I delivered TVs. It was there when I heard there was a vacancy for a photographer at the Mail. I started at the Mail and was taking fifty or sixty photos a week for the *Football Mail* and the *Evening Mail*. As the Mail took other papers over I covered their articles as well. I did the civic reception when Derby won the FA Cup. I stood with the Mayor on the balcony and took the crowd. While we were on the

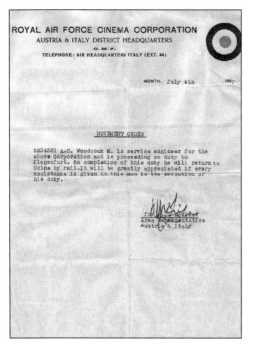

ROYAL AIR FORCE CINEMA CORPORATION
AUSTRIA & ITALY DISTRICT HEADQUARTERS
O. M. F.
TELEPHONE: AIR HEADQUARTERS ITALY (EXT. 44)

MONTH. July 4th   1947

MOVEMENT ORDER

2234381 A.C. Woodcock M. is service engineer for the
above Corporation and is proceeding on duty to
Klagenfurt. On completion of this duty he will return to
Udine by rail.It will be greatly appreciated if every
assistance is given to this man in the execution of
his duty.

Area Representative
Austria & Italy

The Movement Order carried by Maurice at all times.

round ball on the top with a different colour for the day. And so I said, 'I got this lad from school doing work experience. He hasn't got a pass but he's with me.' 'All right, Maurice. It's OK.' They let him take pictures as well. When the Queen Mother was coming into the place they said 'You can go in here.' It was an alcove near the door. I thought, 'Lovely, I'm right here as she gets out the car. I can get a picture of her walking up.' It all happened nicely. Went and got the picture, then she said, 'Oh, you're in your hole are you?' – the Queen Mother, that was. Later on I went inside with them onto the balcony. Harpur-Crewe had got a racehorse on the lawn with a jockey. So I was on the balcony with them. She was talking away because she loves horses and

balcony there were an almighty crash. Some spectators had climbed on the roof of a builders' hut and the roof collapsed. It was the Assembly Rooms being built. I did photos for the shows like Bakewell and Alrewas. I covered the VIP visits. I took Macmillan as he came from the plane. He said, 'I'd best straighten my tie then.' I did Wilson when he was Prime Minister, and the Queen Mother when she met Mr Harpur-Crewe at Calke Abbey. That was before it was open to the public. He was quite a character, Harpur-Crewe was. He'd be cooking his own breakfast in the kitchen when we went. Before the Queen Mother arrived the security service came to check and they all knew me because they'd seen me before at Repton and all that. 'Oh! You're here Maurice?' Got me little pin in me lapel which said you were OK. A little

Maurice Woodcock with the huge spool of 16mm film.

'I'll just straighten my tie, then'. Harold Macmillan arrival at Derby Aviation.

quite, quite nice it was.

Towards the end of my career, this was about thirty-six years at the Mail, I was at the openings of this and that and the other, you know. I was at the ground-breaking for the Octagon Centre when they first started to build. Champagne in the tent, you know. I was at the opening of the Private Hospital on Pastures Hill. What do they call it? Breaking the turf. And then various places. I was at Toyota at the airport and saw all the heads of Japan come in these cars with the councillors but they didn't want to be photographed. Wouldn't have anything. I don't know why but out the car like, they didn't like you doing it. Anyway that was that. That's when it was the last day of the airport. I got an invitation to go and the last flight flew in. I was there with all the planes and everybody before it got turned into Toyota. They had a ceremony. They'd got all marquees on the site. Lavish things. Catering buffets for every nationality. I've never seen anything so lavish. We were all there. 'There you are. Help yourself. What ever you want.' There was a great big fresh salmon. I love fresh salmon. I had a right good tuck in. I think it was Edwina Currie as broke open the barrel with a skin, like, on top. Ladled it out, this drink made from rice for the inaugural ceremony. That was before it was built. I went to the Toyota the first time they were going in the building. They weren't all in the offices then, but the

Managing Director was there. They planted some trees round. Some of the children from school as well. Took me in, showed me where it was. Said 'There's the Director's table in the corner.' They said anyone who wanted to see him, they could go to him without an appointment and say this that and the other. I said 'That's a good idea,' you know and he said to me 'Will you send me some proofs?' Which I did do. Sent him a set. Got a lovely letter back from the chairman of Toyota saying how nice they were.

I carried on at the Burton Mail till I retired at sixty-five. Then I did a column for the Trader called 'Codger's Corner'; it was very popular. I've got all this material, just sitting on it, so I've done videos.

Maurice Woodcock

Railway Goods Porter

The early to mid-fifties was an enjoyable time for me, spent as a full-time student at University. Twelve weeks' holiday in summer needed filling. The last eight were spent working as a goods porter on British Rail.

It was a good arrangement for us both. They needed a general dogsbody; I needed the money. The work was not too taxing mentally. However, the physical effort required enabled me to keep a reasonable level of fitness while pursuing a degree course in physical education. The variety of the work maintained an overall interest; there was rarely a dull moment.

My introduction to goods portering was at No. 2 Warehouse in Derby Street. Here the work was generally handling animal feed,

with Silcocks the main dealer. The roost was ruled by a checker who was a real slave driver. He would off-load a wagon of 1cwt sacks of feed onto the dock unaided. Two or three of us had to keep up with him as we barrowed and stowed them. We had to keep up with him even if the sacks were up to higher floors. These were stowed in double lines usually two, but sometimes three high, if we were short of space. Other work included making up orders for the various farms in the area. This included loading the lorries collecting the consignments.

Derby Street was also the main coal wharf for Burton. We had nothing to do with this traffic, all handling being done by the various coal merchants.

Down the road from No. 2 was No. 4, the bonded warehouse at Derby Turn. I spent a lot of time there. Work was more enjoyable than at No. 2. The pace was more sedate and the greater variety of work added to the interest. The ground floor was bonded, and under the jurisdiction of HM Customs. The whole area was stacked high with casks of whisky, port and sherry. There were also stacks of cases of many different wines and spirits. Most went to Grants, the wine and spirits merchants for Ind Coope.

Incoming traffic came in sealed vans although occasionally pipes of port arrived in open wagons, sheeted over to keep them out of sight. Cases of wine and spirits always came in sealed vans. Whisky came direct from Scottish distillers; sherry and port from Bristol and gin from London.

Unlike the rest of the warehouse, the bonded floor only opened at times set by the customs officers. Before any orders were allowed to leave, the amount of duty had to be calculated and paid. Our job was to collect up the orders and place them ready for inspection. Customs officers dipped the

No. 2 Grain Warehouse in 2001. (P. Williams)

casks to establish the volume while a sample was taken to calculate the gravity. This was used to work out the percentage of alcohol from which the amount of duty to be paid was determined.

When cases of wines and spirits were required the recipients had to list the case numbers. We had to find them and line them up for examination. Once the duty had been paid it was our job to load the orders onto the vehicles that came to collect them.

No. 4 was also responsible for working Horninglow Street Bond. This only opened two mornings a week. Most of the work was concerned with casks, mainly whisky. There was some port and sherry. One job I shall never forget. Working by myself, I actually blended 2,300 gallons of whisky. What a job for a student! It took three of us a couple of mornings to locate all the casks on the list.

This was no easy task. Often the casks we wanted were on the bottom row of a stack of three. Space was at a premium. We did have a fork-lift truck of sorts to help us – a Victorian prototype with a solid iron wheels and a lifting mechanism worked by muscle power. I bet it dated back to when the London and North Western Railway built the warehouse in 1869.

Having found the required casks, we gathered them into a cleared space on the first floor. They were lined up with the shive uppermost. Customs had a sample to determine the alcohol content of each cask, and the volume was also measured. As ever, these measures were required to work out the amount of duty to be paid. Then came the great day. I was told to get on with the blending while my mates started work on another order. The technique was to manoeuvre the cask towards a hole in the floor with the shive uppermost. The shive was knocked out and the cask was rolled forward. The contents, always assuming that I had positioned the cask correctly, poured into the cask. Soon after starting I was soaked to the elbows ands knees with whisky. The job was completed with the addition of two buckets of caramel to give the blend its correct colour. Our side of the job was now complete. The end product went to James Eadie, a former brewery which became wine and spirit merchants for Bass. They bottled it and it was sold in Bass pubs under the Gleneagles label.

Bonded work was only part of the work at No. 4. The first and second floors were used to store barley. This came in van loads from East Anglia. The busiest time was late August and into September. My involvement in this work was minimal. However, when I started work in early July, I was involved in clearing up the previous year's harvest. Bushelling barley was not a particularly pleasant job. The grain had to be gathered in a brass measure called a bushel. A bushel was equivalent of eight gallons; a full sack weighed 1cwt. I never did understand the mysteries attached to weights and measures where grain was concerned! It was heavy work which left you itching all over from the dust. Fortunately the job was done first thing in the morning while it was still cool. The barley went to the breweries where it was turned into malt and used in the brewing process.

The top floor at No. 4 was used for storing dried peas. Like the barley, these came from East Anglia. However, I never saw any leaving the warehouse. I was assured that they were dispatched during the winter to Batchelor's canning factory in Sheffield. Off-loading peas had its own special technique. A van load of peas was shunted adjacent to where the hydraulic rope came through the floors. Three sacks of peas were carefully placed on the track alongside the edge of the dock. The rest were wheeled out of the van and tipped off the dock. They were rolled over the three sacks to land upright on the track ready to be hooked up and hoisted to the top floor for storage – all quite simple and routine.

One morning we were unloading peas from an open wagon, which was unusual. The wagon had been positioned so that the back dropped straight into the wagon. Lifting the sacks up to the top floor was no problem. I was in the wagon hooking up the sacks. As I was waiting for the hook to come down again, I saw, to my horror, my mate. He was supposed to be on the top floor working the hoist. Instead he was coming through the hole above me, head first! He hit the side of the hole. This turned him over and he landed on his feet on the wooden floor of the wagon and finally sat down! I don't know who was more scared, him or me. With a shaking hand, I offered him a cigarette. After a few puffs, he said he was OK and ready to continue. We shifted a few sacks when he called down to say that he would have to go to the office to get his hand bandaged.

That was my cue for a sit down. I was still shaking; thinking of what might have happened. The quiet was disturbed by the sound of heavy footsteps coming along the dock. It was the foreman. He just could not believe what he had heard. He wanted to know the true story. I had to convince him that my mate had really fallen from the top floor into the wagon.

Yes, he had been a very lucky man that day. Any other time we could have been unloading a van. In that case he would have fallen onto the granite sets on the track, rather than having a relatively soft landing on the wooden floor of a wagon. He had indeed fallen from the top floor of No. 4 and had got away with it.

Another station where I spent many an enjoyable hour was at Horninglow Street Goods. This was a permanent six till two shift. The advantage of this was that it enabled you to work overtime during the afternoon. This ensured an enlarged paypacket at the end of the week, something which students could put to good use. The job at Horninglow Street was quite simple. We unloaded the vans that had arrived since the previous day. The contents were put on to an electric trolley which transferred them to the dray which would take them to their destination in various parts of the town. These were hauled by the three wheeled mechanical horses which were a feature of railway town deliveries in the 1950s.

Later in the morning the mechanical horses would arrive back with collections for despatch all over the country. Some were full loads, i.e. big enough to fill a van which would be sent direct to its destination. Most, however, ended up in mixed loads which were sent to Derby St Mary's for further sorting to make full loads to a single destination. Throughout the morning the whole goods shed was a hive of activity as the various parcels were hand-sorted and sent their way. Things quietened down as the shift drew to a close. By 2 p.m. the day's work was done.

A number of overtime jobs were available for the afternoon. Wetmore

Bank was a frequent location. This was on the east side of the main line between Wetmore Railway Bridge and the junction into Horninglow Street Goods and Hawkins Lane Loco Shed. All the incoming loads of empty beer casks that came to the bank had to be sorted to make up loads for the separate breweries. Loads labelled to specific breweries were sent on after a quick look to make sure there were no foreigners inside. Sorting casks had its own particular skill. The ability to roll a cask out of an open wagon into the next wagon saved a lot of time. This was important as the basis of payment for the work was either piece-work or bonus.

At the end of the days work the checker in charge worked out how much we were to be paid. A lively discussion always took place over whether we should claim bonus payment or overtime. I never did follow these arguments. Suffice to say, I was always satisfied with the outcome.

Another job at Wetmore Bank was wagon cleaning. Empty wagons destined for the beer traffic had to be cleaned. Wagons with oil or grease on the floor or sides were not acceptable. Others required a sweep out and would then be OK. These empties came from all over the country to meet the requirements of the breweries. This was understandable when hundreds of wagons were required daily to carry beer to destinations all over the country.

One hot afternoon I remember I had the misfortune to have a line of empties which had come from Derby. Many had been used for carrying newly made bricks. Apart from the odd brick end, the floor was covered in a thick layer of brick dust. It was not until I started to shovel it out

The coal face. Many Burton men worked down the pits. There were no pit head showers then. Men returned home at the end of a shift covered in coal dust and would scrub down in the scullery.

of the wagon that I learned how heavy brick dust could be. I'm sure the regular gang on the bank had saved them for me! With fraying temper and sweat pouring out of me, the situation called for desperate measures. I must admit to using rather a lot of 'dirty' labels that afternoon!

On rare occasions you had a job that really sticks out in the memory. A very happy afternoon was spent on the sheet dray. This was a lorry and trailer job. Every so often it was decided by the powers that be, that all of the wagon sheets that had accumulated in the various brewery sites had to be collected. A number of sites were visited and a lot of

sheets were collected. At each site we were the 'guests' and the hospitality of our hosts knew no bounds. I don't quite know how much ale was consumed that afternoon. It was, however, a very happy student that cycled home that tea-time!

Another job I did, and only on one occasion, was to go to a small wooden warehouse which I believed was formerly owned by the Great Northern Railway. This was towards Wetmore Road and was not to be confused with the GN Grain Warehouse. The job was to unload bottles. These had come from the manufacturers. I never did find out their ultimate destination. I assume that they were for the breweries. Well who else would want green half-pint-sized bottles with narrow necks! There must have been thousands stored there.

Yes, railway work during the 1950s in the Goods Department was an enjoyable way to occupy a long summer holiday. The variety of work at the various stations meant that you came across a lot of interesting characters. But the work was not confined to Burton. Unloading flour at Barton under Needwood was a relaxing job, while general goods work at Swadlincote was a little more arduous. But that is another story.

Peter Williams

Fred's Snippet

My parents always kept fowls and two pigs. At Christmas my mother reared her own cockerels. She was well known for this. They would weigh around 10 or 12lb and people wondered how she did it. My elder brothers worked at the brewery and brought their beer allowance home in a bottle. Sometime before Christmas my mother used to mix the cockerels' feed with beer instead of water. They were then put inside a small pen. They were always asleep. That is why they made such big birds.

Early Working Days

Tuesday 7 August 1956 – not a particularly notable day you might think, but it was for me. It was the day I started work. I had been fortunate enough to pass the eleven-plus at junior school (Belmont Street, Swadlincote) and go on to Ashby Boys' Grammar School which I had expected to attend till the age of sixteen years and then hopefully go on to university or college. However owing to family circumstances I decided to leave school at fifteen and start earning a living.

As my last school term was coming to an end I scoured the Situations Vacant columns of the Burton *Daily Mail* but saw nothing I either fancied or could do and was thinking that perhaps I would be going back to Ashby in September after all. Then one night I saw an advert for a junior clerk in a travel agency which was to open shortly in Burton. I had never heard of the company – Frames' Tours Ltd – and did not know much about travel agents either. There had never been a proper travel agent in Burton before although there had been a shipping agent.

Anyway off went my letter of application, in my best handwriting, and by return of post came a reply asking me to go for an interview. The interview was with Mr Roy Johnson, manager designate of the office, and took place in the actual office situated at No. 14 Market Place, Burton on Trent. This was the first job interview I had ever experienced. Everything seemed to go well and a few days later a letter arrived offering me the position of junior clerk at the princely wage of £2 10s per week subject to satisfactory references. Such references were forthcoming and so my working life commenced.

On that first day the staff consisted of the aforementioned Roy Johnson and me! His wife Pat joined us later as part-time shorthand typist. They came from

Northampton.

The office had not been fitted out so we started off working on any available surface and my first job was stamping our name and address on to the various leaflets etc. so that prospective travellers would know where to make their booking. A few days later the shop fitters arrived (Broughton & Moore of Blackpool) and set to work. When they had finished what a smart place they had created. Light oak panelling abounded together with a similar counter and matching furniture. In those days staff stood on their side of the counter and clients on the other although seats were available for the latter whilst they were waiting for attention.

Frames is still fondly remembered by many because it was a proper travel agency and not just a holiday shop which is all that is generally available nowadays. We were agents for British Railways, most shipping companies, principal airlines and many holiday companies. In addition we booked tickets for London theatres, any travelling circuses visiting the area and could obtain foreign currency and travellers cheques. We also operated our own holidays to the Continent and in the British Isles. On reflection the only thing we did not do was to book tickets for express coach services although this was undertaken eventually.

It must be remembered that the Second World War had only finished some ten years earlier and the destinations available for 'package holidays' were not very extensive or far flung either. Furthermore, stringent currency regulations applied and at one point the maximum amount allowed was £10 per person, so most people still holidayed in the British Isles.

A big part of our business in the early days was rail travel and it was dealing with this where I had my first contact with the public. No formal training was given; everything was learnt by watching and listening. I soon found that in Roy Johnson I had an excellent tutor. To be honest I did not have much knowledge of the railway network but fortunately I found it very interesting and soon became adept at dealing with enquiries for the remotest destinations. We could also make bookings to destinations in continental Europe via the cross channel ferries and connecting express trains such as the Golden Arrow, Orient Express etc.

Holiday camps were at the height of their popularity at that time and every year we booked literally hundreds of Burton and South Derbyshire folk to Butlins, Pontins, Squires Gate, Middleton Towers, Prestatyn and various other camps. At this time Butlins gave a reduction of 7s 6d per person per week to parties of 'four young ladies or four young men' occupying the same chalet. How ironic that in later years parties of this nature were banned by Butlins!

Coach tours were enjoyed by many people and in those days were still licensed by the Traffic Commissioners and could only be booked at agents authorised by the operating company. Midland Red, Trent and Worthingtons were allowed to pick up in Burton but Frames could only book for Worthingtons. The Trent booking agents were Darleys Bookshop in High Street and Mr Richards at Derby Turn post office whilst Midland Red had their own office in Station Street, run for many years by Mrs June Lowe. In later years all three companies were to become part of the National Bus Company so we were eventually agents for all three. Frames was quite a large company and ran its own coaches as well. All the year round we did London Sightseeing Tours and in the summer coach tours of Great Britain and Ireland.

There was not much – if any – 'technology' in use at that time. Most bookings were done by post without recourse even to the telephone! Imagine it nowadays going into a local holiday shop to book your fortnight in the sun and being told 'we'll let you know in about a week' but that's the way it was forty-five years ago and nobody complained!

Such long-distance travel as there was usually meant going by sea. Air travel was very costly and Frames were agents for all the well known shipping lines. Some are still with us such as Cunard and P&O. Others are only memories– Canadian Pacific, Union Castle, Royal Mail, Shaw Savill, Blue Star, French Line; the list seems endless and there are dozens more.

I found I had an aptitude for the job and found it both interesting and rewarding. Much encouragement was given by Mr Frame but I really owe such a lot to my first boss Roy Johnson. His knowledge was great and it was somewhat of a blow when he moved on after some two years to open another new branch at Hemel Hempstead. He could be a hard taskmaster and stern when necessary – indeed he told me in later years that he used to give me a good telling off every week whether I needed it or not just to keep me on my toes. I'm sure I was none the worse for it!

The next manager, Les Hawkins, also came from Northampton so routines and procedures didn't change much. He also stayed for about two years. By this time the staff had increased and I was now senior clerk and able to take charge in the manager's absence. We also had a full-time shorthand typist. Still not much technology, but we were now using the phone to make bookings and we were still the only travel agency in Burton and South Derbyshire. Not that we were complacent; we took a pride in our work and no booking was too small or too large.

Les Hawkins' successor was a bit of a disaster. Mr Frame made one of his visits and was less than impressed with what he saw and heard. The outcome was that the incumbent was dismissed shortly after and yours truly appointed manager. I was twenty years of age and the youngest manager the company had ever had – I felt very proud! I had been virtually running the office for several months but was now thrown in at the deep end. I was called to London to see Mr Frame who gave me much advice which I have never forgotten.

By this time more and more long distance travel was by plane. Sea travel was very much on the decline although cruises were making up some of the shortfall. Most planes were still propeller-driven as not many pure jets were in use. The UK had two state airlines–BEA serving Europe and the British Isles and BOAC covering the rest of the world. The former operated Dakotas, Elizabethans and Viscounts amongst others and the latter included Stratocruisers, DC7C's, Argonauts and Britannias in its fleet.

As many local people will recall, there

was an airport at Burnaston (where the Toyota factory now stands) and Derby Airways flew hundreds of passengers each summer to a variety of destinations. The planes operated included Marathons, Dakotas and Doves. In those far-off days the airport did not function during winter months. The runway was grass: take-off and landing was novel, to say the least. My first flight was from Burnaston to Jersey and back in the same day. It must have been summer 1957 and was definitely in an eighteen-seater Miles Marathon which had four engines and a chemical toilet – what an experience!

We booked great numbers of package holidays both within the British Isles and to Europe. There were no holidays to any far-off or exotic destinations then as air travel was still in its infancy. People did not get such long holidays either and many employers insisted on a 'compulsory fortnight' which was at the end of July or beginning of August. Most holidays to the continent were by rail and sea so for the farther away destinations you used up a fortnight but could go no farther than say Italy or mainland Spain. You couldn't go to Majorca or Greece! Frames operated their own holidays and were agents for many other companies, most no longer in business. Names that come into mind are WTA, Swans, LeRoy, Poly Travel, Sir Henry Lunn, Fourways, Horizon, Blue Cars, Lyons, Global/Overland, Gaytours, Smiths, Happiways, Spencers. To go back to air travel I should have mentioned that flying boats were still operating in the fifties and I well remember booking a local couple with Aquila Airways from Southampton to Madeira. Other airlines from those times include British Eagle,

What a way to travel! The charabanc.

Building starts on the Riverside Hotel at Branston, with a view across the river to Drakelow Power Station.

Airwork, Hunting Clan, Silver City, DanAir, Skyways, Starways, Jersey Airlines, Olley Air Services.

I was at Burton for over twenty years, during which time the amount of trade grew amazingly in spite of the fact that many other travel agencies opened up. We experienced good times and bad. The four-day week and devaluation of the pound spring to mind, but in spite of all this we managed to continue and prosper. At the end of 1981 I achieved a personal ambition: the office turnover for that year just exceeded £1 million. Not bad for a small office with a staff of six, four full-time and two part-time.

In January 1982 I moved to the Derby branch- but that's another story.

Keith West

CHAPTER 6
Elements

Sinai House. (D. Bonnett)

Landscape

Natural landscape arises from a combination of geology and climate but what we see today is largely the result of human activity, which enables it to be used as another source of local history. In many cases this can be seen by visual observation.

In geological terms we are living in the Holocene Epoch, which began about 10,000 years ago when the ice sheets receded northwards from a line passing through Wexford, Aberaeron and High Wycombe. Climatic changes during the epoch have been considerable, causing afforestation and soil creation by about 3000 BC, followed by a cool period until around 200 BC, after which it gradually became warmer.

Burton upon Trent is situated in the north-east corner of the triangular Midland Plain, where the valley narrows to a width of about 1 mile. The river and its flood-plain occupy the eastern side at the foot of steeply rising ground. The main part of the town lies in the larger part of the flat valley floor which is at an altitude of between 145 and 155ft. In Roman times one of their main roads, Rykneild Street, passed through on the west side, having crossed the Trent at Alrewas, where the valley is also flat, but wider.

The two upland areas either side are significant features. To the west is the plateau known as Needwood Forest which once covered the whole area between the rivers Blithe, Dove and Trent. It is generally at an altitude of between 450 and 500ft, with a steep scarp slope in the vicinity of Lawn's Farm, near Tatenhill. The plateau contains the deposits of Tutbury gypsum, hydrated calcium sulphate, which made the Burton waters famous for brewing.

The landscape of Burton and district during medieval times has left some visible remains for those prepared to look, but one of its most striking features, the 'Great Bridge of Burton', where a battle was fought in 1322, was regrettably destroyed in the nineteenth century. However, Monk's Bridge over the Dove near Egginton still survives although subject to recent damage. In the town there are still buildings which contain parts of original timber frames or roofs from the fourteenth century.

Tutbury Castle ruins are a well-known feature of the local landscape but perhaps less well known are two short sections of its Pale; one section either side of Chatsworth Drive and another running north-west off Park Lane.

Although all the districts around the town were important in its development the most significant was arguably Needwood Forest and not only for its gypsum deposits. Its influence extended as far west as Abbots Bromley and included what became known as Sinai Park, which also had connections with the Abbey. There is probably nothing left of the forest as it was at Domesday or even when designated a Royal Forest in 1339. The forest had a number of ancient hamlets and villages at its edges, all of which had some effect and dependency on it. One of the oldest and least affected by changes in recent times is Tatenhill, which nestles in a small valley or dingle running down to the Trent valley floor.

Several factors contributed to the final loss of the forest after the seventeenth century, remembering that by this time limited clearances, both legal and otherwise, had been going on for some time. As a result of Charles II's debts (he being the then Duke of Lancaster), 25,000 trees were felled between 1697 and 1701 and during the eighteenth century many more were felled illegally. Most trees were cut down and straight roads with wide verges laid across the forest. The landscape is now characterized by geometrical fields, quick set hedges and drainage ditches.

The Civil War was a setback to the town. Its economic state was probably a factor in Lord Paget's promotion of the 1699 Trent Navigation Act, the works for which were completed in 1712, making Burton the furthest inland port on the river.

Commercial brewing began after the Navigation was open, firstly in Horninglow Street in the 1720s. The fine Georgian buildings which still exist there are a legacy of this period. The medieval parish church was also rebuilt between 1720 and 1726. Later, around 1780, the Peel family built cotton mills at Bond End, powered by water via the new 'Peel's Cut' off the river. Although now sifted up, its route can be followed as a feature on the ground. The cotton industry was the town's biggest employer for nearly sixty years but despite this and the opening of Brindley's Grand Junction Canal in 1777, the population in 1801 was only 6,000. The mushroom growth did not begin until after the arrival of the first railway in 1839. This transformed the landscape as the breweries spread westwards over the ancient withies, crofts and moors. The canal created a small new community at Horninglow Wharf where the change to a narrow canal occurred, but the buildings have now gone, remembered only by the model at the Bass Museum.

John Bonnett

Water Under the Bridge

If we use a little imagination, and strip away the 'superstructure' of modern Burton for a moment, we see a landscape profile which is essentially the product of the most recent Ice Age. Of course, over a period of thousands of years, some considerable modification has occurred, but the climatic change we talk of today is relatively small compared with the comings and goings of the major glacial periods.

It is difficult to contemplate the timescale required by the various erosion agents to make a difference to the landscape, but every time we have an extreme rainfall event, the process of erosion and deposition continues.

Measurement of the various behaviour patterns within the atmosphere has been

River Dove flooding at Rolleston Cricket ground, February 1977 (D. Stanier)

Snowmelt led to River Trent floods in January 1988, seen from near St Modwen's church. (D. Stanier)

possible with the aid of scientific instruments for about three centuries. By the mid-nineteenth century weather observation had become a popular activity and in the, by then, well-established town of Burton upon Trent detailed records of rainfall were maintained.

John Matthews had a rain gauge in operation at Winshill by at least 1865, and just ten years later, Bass Brewers began a rainfall record at Shobnall. In 1876, the newly appointed Headmaster at Burton Grammar School, C. Upton Tripp, set up a comprehensive weather observation station. He had already published rainfall figures in earlier years while at Trent College, Nottingham.

On the Needwood plateau, to the west of Burton, W. Bennett began rainfall observation at Rangemore in 1866. His record continued for the next fifty-three years. At nearby Byrkley Lodge, the commercially operated Needwood Gardens (later known as Brykley Gardens) also boasted a comprehensive weather station by at least 1885. This continued until 1957, several years after the Lodge itself was demolished.

The municipal authority in Burton also operated a weather station, and it became the normal procedure for water authorities to operate rain gauges fairly widely. It is therefore safe to assume that throughout the twentieth century, someone, somewhere in the vicinity of the town, maintained accurate weather records of one sort or another. The writer commenced a local observation record in 1970.

The state of the weather is often the first topic of conversation when two people meet, and as Burton is situated in close proximity to one of the major river systems of England, so the condition of the Trent has also played a hand during the history of the town. Rainfall is therefore one of the more important weather phenomena to consider. The catchment of the Trent itself, and the numerous watercourses flowing into it upstream from Burton, covers a large part of the North-west Midlands. However, as far as Burton is concerned, at valley level, the annual average rainfall may fluctuate between about 25.5in and 26.5in. At the time of writing, the latest standard thirty-year mean (1971-2000) is towards the upper end that range. A short series of very wet years (1998-2000) has contributed to this situation.

Although in any period of thirty years, a wide range of extremes will be experienced, we still have to go back to the nineteenth century to find both the driest and wettest years on record for the town (i.e. since 1865). The most severe 'drought' years produce annual totals of less than 20in of rain. 1887 had only 17.2in. This exceptionally dry year occurred just fifteen years after the wettest. 1872 stands out in this respect with 38.5in. That year is regarded as having been the wettest in the British Isles for more than 250 years. In Burton, few years have exceeded 35in of rain, and the most recent

Brookside, Rolleston, during a severe cold spell, December 1981. (D. Stanier)

Andressey Bridge, November 2000. We all remember this flood. (R. Tipper)

approach was in 2000.

The wettest months can produce 5 or 6in of rain, and these do not always relate to the more thundery months of summer. February 1977 produced 6.5in of rain, this being the wettest month in recent years. The River Trent was in a state of flood for a week during that month. But, it was the very thundery July of 1915 which holds the record, with 7.8in.

Sometimes, we may experience 1 or even 2in of rain within a 24-hour period. In some exceptionally heavy thundery downpours, 3 or even 4in may be possible. Such events usually lead to damaging flash floods. Another form of precipitation associated with thunderstorms is hail, and on 14 July 1975, parts of Burton and nearby Stretton were affected by a brief, but very damaging fall of large hail. Many hailstones of an inch across fell in this, but the extreme examples were up to 2in wide.

In a typical year, 172 days will produce measurable rain. In the wettest years 200 can be exceeded, and, in the driest just under 150 may be recorded.

Included in rainfall data are the winter snowfalls. An inch of rain would equate to about one foot of level snow, but Burton rarely experiences snowfalls of this magnitude. Some of the winters of the early 1940s, and most famously 1947, probably achieved snow depths of this order.

The overall warming trend has led to a much reduced incidence of snowfall in the most recent ten year period.

David Stanier

Fred's Snippet

Milroy the milkman used to dress his horse and float with flags and bunting on St George's day and special occasions. He was also a weather man and he would tell everyone what the weather was going to be whilst on his rounds.

Floods, November 2000. This building on Meadow Road off the Trent Bridge stood on the Old Burton Bridge as seen on page 4. (R. Tipper)

The floods in Guild Street. (T. Garner)

Town Centre Floods

Growing up in Guild Street, Burton, in what was basically at the time the town centre, in the late 1950s and early 1960s, meant we had to experience what is now virtually unheard of; that is, flooding to the streets.

We lived at No. 32 Guild Street, one of a row of terraced houses (known to all as the Fire Brigade Cottages) belonging to Bass Brewery that stood on the west side of the street between the Guild Tavern Public House and the entrance gateway to Bass weighbridge and fire station.

My father at the time was employed as a delivery driver and a part-time fireman with the Brewery, the rented house going with the job, which as well as turning out on fire calls within the brewery site meant they

96

were put on stand-by whenever the Corporation Fire Service went out on a 999 call. As soon as there was a prolonged heavy rainfall all eyes would be focused on the roadway in front of the houses for all the tell-tale signs of the water starting to back up from the drains.

If any plans had been made to go out these were always put on hold, everyone knowing that if the rain persisted then eventually there would be a knock on the door from a member of Bass Engineers' Department telling everybody that 'the floods are up again' and to get the flood boards out.

Each house was provided with two of these boards, one for the front door and one for the back door. These were pieces of timber roughly 2in thick and 18in to 2ft deep that slotted into permanent grooves fixed to the outer frames of the front and back door. Sand bags were then placed across the bottom edges and up the sides for added defence.

The houses were built so that when the floods usually peaked, the water would be just above pavement height at the front, but at the back door would be about 2ft deep, making trips to the toilet out of the question for a few hours at least, unless you were prepared to don Wellington boots for the trip down the yard. There were no inside toilets in those days.

I remember vividly one time when I was quite young my parents taking me to a visiting circus appearing down Wellington Street Extension, when during the performance there was an announcement that anyone living in the town centre area should return home immediately as the floods were starting to come up. We dashed home but as this entailed walking the length

Enjoying the sunshine in the paddling pool at Shobnall playing fields.

The outdoor swimming pool belonging to the Working Men's Club on Stapenhill Road. (M. Wright)

of the Extension then to the Town Hall to catch a corporation bus into town, getting off outside the County Court in Station Street, then along Guild Street, we were too late. The water had entered the house, so rugs and furniture were ruined.

We moved in the early 1960s as my father took another job and it was around this time that the River Trent was dredged and the drainage system improved, putting an end to all but spasmodic flooding of the area.

Terry Garner

A Walk Through History

It was May 1940. I was twenty-two. I was in a house in Calais with two other soldiers, all of us armed with just rifles. We were waiting

there supposedly to stop the German Army, if it chose to advance up that street. The floor of the house was on fire but that was of little consequence in that situation. Looking round the room, I saw a map on the sideboard and I put it in my jacket. A few hours later forty of us were in a building near the harbour. An officer came in and said, 'There's a German tank round the corner. Has anyone got a grenade?' We gave a grim laugh. None of us had ever seen a grenade.

Two days later we were in a long column staggering along a road through woods, with German guards on either side. We were staggering because we had been marched a long way with very little food. I staggered round a bush and fell into it. Soon I was alone and all was quiet. I went to a French house nearby and begged some food. Then I looked at the map. It was the map of that area. For the next month, I had an adventurous time following the map to the coast, walking mostly by night.

It was May 1988. I was still fascinated by maps and history. I had been walking in the countryside around Burton and I had found some attractive and very interesting places. I could see on the map footpaths that led from Shobnall Road to Tatenhill, then on to Dunstall, and on to Highland Park, along Cuckoo Cage Lane back to Tatenhill and Shobnall Road.

So I set off from near the Albion on Shobnall Road and was soon struggling up a very steep hill. I walked on 200 yards and found myself looking at a derelict half-timbered Elizabethan house. There were chickens running in and out. I was astonished but then realized that this was Sinai House, an ancient outpost of Burton Abbey. The view from there was staggering. I was looking over the town to

Winshill, to Winshill water tower, and beyond Drakelow to Rosliston. I closed my eyes and tried to imagine that I was a monk in 1300 looking at a very different picture. Down below I would have seen a wooded valley with the shining Trent meandering through it. I would have seen a small town but extensive buildings of the Abbey which had been founded in AD 1000 and grown very prosperous. I would have seen people and carts passing along the old Roman Road-Rykneld Street (now the A38).

A week later I walked through Bretby Park. In 1630 the finest gardens in England were laid out here. Lord Stanhope also arranged for the dams to be constructed that created the stair of lakes still here. I passed the lakes and went through Hoofies Wood, down to the road at Noah's Ark. Half-a-mile further on, I turned right across a bridge over Repton Brook and saw a series of cascades. I could not imagine how they came to be there. The answer, when I found it, was quite unbelievable. Sir Vauncy Harpur-Crewe, of Calke Abbey, had let a house to his cousin. Some time later Sir Vauncy with his gamekeeper was running across the lawn of the house, chasing butterflies. The cousin appeared and objected to them invading his privacy. Sir Vauncy was furious. A couple of days later he returned with all his men and all his wagons-and knocked the house down! So now we can see the cascades, the lake, the avenue of trees, but the big house has gone. This place is shown on the map as Lawn Bridge, but the local people call it Robin's Cross. They say that local tradition has it that Robin Hood came this way, on his way to tournaments at Ashby Castle. Did he cross the Trent at Newton Solney?

The cascades. (H. Ward)

A friend took me round the area to show me that paths and tracks linked up to suggest that there was an ancient road leading to Newton Solney and some records talk of a ford across the Trent at that village. I know someone who lived there and I asked him if he knew anything about the ford in the river, and he laughed me to scorn. A week later he told me that he had met an old lady in the village, who years ago, had indeed walked across the river at that point.

A day or two later, I was walking on from Noah's Ark and the cascades, to follow a footpath that led from the road to Bretby village. As I passed along the edge of a field, I stopped to wonder why there was a ditch 20 yards wide. If I had been trained to read the signs of the countryside, I would have known what it was. As it was,

The high wall at Dunstall. (H. Ward)

I had to wait until I found an old booklet all about Bretby, which told me that the ditch was a medieval road, leading from Bretby castle to Repton (when there were probably no other roads in the area).

I wanted to complete the Tatenhill walk so I came down Battlestead Hill into Tatenhill and went on to Dunstall – a lovely village. Approaching Dunstall, I passed by a high wall with a chimney on top, quite an incongruous sight. I did not know what this was. The chimney was at the end of long flues that ran right across the wall. There would have been a fireplace at the far end so heat in the wall warmed apricots and peaches trained against it. However, when I went into the grounds and looked along the inside of the wall, there was something that did puzzle me. There were four small shapes, now bricked up, that had obviously been openings or gratings. What was their purpose?

In the reign of Edward I, Sir Philip de Somerville, of Wychnor Hall, granted some land at Dunstall to Hugh, son of Walter Newbold, and his wife, on condition that they rendered to him eight hens at Christmas. They also had to provide him on the feast of St John the Baptist (24 June) with a nosegay of white or red roses; with the roses they had to help him decorate the 'bacon'. This was the famous Flitch kept through the centuries at Wychnor Hall for any couple who could prove they had been happily married for a year. No one has ever won it! A picture of the flitch still hangs in Wychnor Hall, now a country club.

I saw on the map that there were possible circular walks from Tutbury Castle. So one day I set off to go to Fauld, Hanbury, Capertition Wood, Hares Holes Rough, Castle Hayes Farm and back to Tutbury. I passed close to Queen's Purse Wood and the gypsum works, and across fields to find myself looking down into the crater – the crater caused by that enormous explosion in 1944 – of 4,000 tons of bombs!

A fellow member of Burton-on-Trent Golf Club was in that explosion and lived to tell the tale. He was an artificer sent to check up on the working practices there. Along with an officer, he entered the underground galleries and they made their way to the main workshops – a large underground cavern. They were absolutely horrified! Men were working dismantling bombs and shells. They should have been working in isolated compartments, so that any explosion would be confined to a small area – but they were all working together! They should have been using copper chisels that would not cause sparks – but they were using steel chisels! So my friend and the officer agreed that they would have to make changes as soon as possible. Then they went back towards the entrance to inspect other departments. My friend was standing at the door of a storeroom when an enormous blast blew him inside and saved his life. That explosion blew two farms into the air with all the people, the cattle, the houses, the barns, the machinery to disappear entirely. To look down into the crater even today makes one shudder.

Another day I followed a second walk from Tutbury. A walk that led me along Alder Brook, across the meadows to lovely Brookside in Rolleston, and across more fields to see the great water wheel at Tutbury Mill. Soon I arrived at Tutbury Bridge, over the River Dove. This was the scene of frenzied activity in 1831, when local people began finding countless silver coins along the river bank. Five hundred years before that the Earl of Lancaster, fleeing from the battle of Burton Bridge, forded the river here. In doing so, he lost his war chest in the river. He never had a chance to reclaim it because he was caught and executed soon afterwards.

Some time later I was walking from Rolleston to Coton-in-the-Elms and Edingale. Alas it is Coton-without-the-Elms now, all struck down by Dutch elm disease. This village once belonged to Burton Abbey, on condition that the Abbot supplied a hound on a leash to the King, whenever he visited Derbyshire. I went along the side of Pessall Brook and past Raddle Farm to Edingale. I wanted to cut off from here to go to Croxall, a couple of miles away. It's easy to go through Croxall without a second thought, but Croxall is a very interesting place. You can stand and gaze in awe at Croxall Hall – a beautiful seventeenth-century building with a remarkable topiary.

At Croxall the map shows the site of a medieval village and a 'motte'. A motte is usually a mound on which fortifications were built (a wooden stockade or a castle). But this mound has been identified as a Saxon burial place. That is Croxall's historical heritage. But there's a romantic story here too. In the church is the memorial tablet to Ann Beatrix Horton. The Horton family have lived in nearby Catton hall since 1405. Lady Ann acquired great fame because she is the lady Lord Byron was describing when he wrote the poem beginning: 'She walks in beauty like the night / Of cloudless climes and starry skies' He saw her at a ball wearing a black dress, starred with spangles, and was so entranced that he sat up all night to write the poem.

There's a lot of pleasure to be had from walking through the countryside, admiring the views, looking at the trees and flowers; from making your way through the woods, looking at dappled sunk-light, listening for woodpeckers, glorying the blue haze of bluebells, scenting the wild garlic or the honeysuckle. But you are missing a lot if you pass on without thinking of all the stories of your surroundings. Just think of all the people who have been there before you – the Ancient Britons, the Romans, the Saxons or Danes, the serf, the miner,

the ploughman, the forester, the soldier – all have left their mark. Almost every place has a story: farms, lanes, rivers, roads, hills, fields. Yes, even fields. There's a field at Overseal called Dead Danes Bottom because remains were found there of a battle long ago.

But the reality is that around Burton there is a wealth of local history; from the common place to the comic; from the romantic to the ridiculous; from the intriguing to the incredible.

Holly Ward

An aerial view of the Trent Bridge. The stray dogs' home can be seen on the Island and the old swimming baths are at the top in the centre. PC Wilf Watkins used to feed the dogs; he was a police champion boxer.

Cows now graze where the dogs' home used to be. A view looking east from the site of the Victorian Public Swimming Baths. See the water tower? (D. Stanier)

The arrival of the Burton Sea Cadets' very first boat. It was previously a ship's lifeboat. (H. Cox)

Musings of a Stapenhill Lad

Turning left out of the back door, nine paces found the outside toilet. Indoors the black-leaded open fire range provided many changes of air per hour, and produced a draughty environment. No carpets, no television, no car outside, no holidays away from home, no central heating.

Positives included the River Trent, the wasteland round the corner for cricket or football, Burton Baths against the Trent Bridge weir and the four cinemas. Osier beds in Short Street were conveniently close to the orchard where we all scrumped in late summer.

Hopscotch, conkers, lamp-post climbing and train spotting occupied many. Hanging by one's feet beneath the wall-top railings of Short Street School, alternately touching toes and ground strengthened our stomach muscles and added to the fun. When we felt really grown-up on our way to Hill Street Boys' School we would put a penny in the machine at Lovatt's shop and get two cigarettes and two matches in a packet. Crayols I believe they were called.

Uncle Reg lived next door. His pride and joy was a Calthorpe motorcycle which he would carefully service outside. Being a yeomanry member of the Territorial Army he still wore puttees and a bandolier, very smart too. Uncle Bill, an elderly miner and mines rescue man, used lamps on his cycle which operated on carbide (acetylene). My job was to fetch it. Oil lamps were widely used on the railways and many cyclists, myself included, fitted these to our cycles. If you had the 'King of the Road' type you were posh!

Pigeon lofts were commonplace. Going into town was to 'Go down Burton', coal was in a 'coal-ole'. Clothes were washed (more commonly 'weshed') in a copper, which was usually made of steel. Fuel was 'firing'; 'canna' and 'wunna' were used for cannot and will not.

Mr Dobson of Dobson's boatyard would assess your ability before allowing you aboard his boats, whether a skiff or the heavier six-seater. Go upstream and you had to tug the boat across the weir, now long gone, which was opposite Bill Sherratts farm.

It was common practice when one was young to give up your seat on public transport to a lady or elderly person. It seems a great pity to me that buses are not manned by two people today. One very cheerful conductor used to consistently laugh and joke with most passengers, and identified some stops in Burton with 'Hyde Park Corner' or 'Oxford Street.' However he didn't suffer any misbehaviour lightly!

Thursday at four o'clock saw those who wished to swim, walk from Hill Street to the public baths. Bob Ingley, one of our number, being high spirited and braver than the rest, would walk over the steel girder work of Andressey Bridge – in both directions.

After much talk of the event, war came on 3 September 1939. Neville Chamberlain's announcement came via our old Gamages radio on what was a beautiful summery day. For once the weather didn't help since we had all seen newsreel pictures of the German planes bombing Spanish cities during the civil war in that country.

One of the many traditions which we have lost since that time relates to funerals. When the bereaved assembled for the funeral, all close neighbours would draw their curtains across as a sign of sympathy and understanding. Curtains remained closed until the cortège had departed. Similarly, when any cortège passed a uniformed serviceman or policeman, the man would stand at the kerbside and salute. Hats were removed by others as a sign of respect.

I moved to Broadway Central School in 1940 where our first teacher was Miss M. Smith. Other names I remember include Miss Harper, Pa Phillips, Arthur Ormerod and the Head, Mr Bristow. My pals and I took advantage of a very new, pretty teacher by hosing down the toilet area during the lunch break. Caught out, we suffered the inevitable punishment which would have had some of today's parents running for Messrs Watchit, Scratchit and Ditchit, barristers of this parish! We got what we deserved! Bob Ingley, whose form teacher the lovely lady was, would advise her each day on whether the seams of her stockings were straight! Unsolicited advice though it was, ladies did like to know these things. Seams in those days could have been the real thing or painted on to suit.

Deep trenches were dug in the Heath Road Recreation Ground to be used as protection against air attack. Later, as the large square brick and concrete shelters became available, (many in residential streets) the trenches were infilled. Drakelow Park was ploughed and planted with vegetables, in common with any other stretches of open land suitable for that purpose. Permanent notices under the defence regulations were affixed at the entrances to these sites warning of very severe penalties for stealing or damaging crops.

In late May 1941, the pride of Britain's fleet, the battle-cruiser HMS *Hood*, was sunk by the guns of the German *Bismarck* in the North Atlantic. Our form master told a small group of us this during a morning stand easy, and I reckon that was one of the most shocking items of news I had heard.

Looking for a joinery apprenticeship, Bass brewery offered me work in their Railway Office which was in the Middle Brewery. The office boss was Bill Whetton, with Les Harris and Mr Large as senior figures. Harold Stockwell and Don Bacon were the young members. One other elderly man whose name escapes me, used to walk to the High Street club each lunch time, informing us that he drank his Red Label straight from the bottle. This seemed incongruous since he had moved up from the Portsmouth office due to the wartime conditions, and would wear a very fine dark overcoat, bowler hat, spats and yellow gloves. He was inseparable from his furled umbrella carried exclusively on his left arm. Contrasts with the brewery workers as he walked through the Middle Yard prompted great mirth and remarks until he became part of the scene. We three younger types had great sport by attaching a length of string to the very large

drawer of the slightly built Les Harris, and tightening it by a deft knee movement so that the poor bloke struggled endlessly to get it open. Don left first to go into the light blues, Harold and finally myself left to go into the dark blues. When one day Bill Whetton's daughter Hilary, a serving Wren, bounced into the office full of good cheer, complete with her young Royal Navy officer friend, before she got to put her arms round Bill he exploded: 'Put that cigarette out'. Rules were rules with Bill. He was a disciplinarian, but he did have a good and human side.

Surrounded by around thirty level-crossings, a fleet of steam engines, and scores of boiler chimneys, our town centre was often hazy and overcast. Pollution was awful at that time, but fighting the war (and getting the beer out) was a total priority. November 1944, sitting on my high stool, the earth seemed to move, looking out toward the New Brewery chimneys (the Brewhouse was part of that brewery), two chimneys were apparently moving in a sine wave fashion throughout their length! We exchanged glances and were silent for a few seconds. Surely we didn't have earthquakes in Britain? We heard nothing, but then why should we, being in the centre of a busy and very noisy brewery? RAF Fauld had exploded. It is said that 4,000 tons of bombs had detonated. Rumours abounded, but the official enquiry offers the most logical explanation of an accidental cause. Ideas that a V rocket targeted and hit Fauld are absurd. Another relative of mine, Uncle Jim, a miner and trained mines rescue man, spent a week at the mine helping the many others on site. Visiting the mine during my working life, I recall seeing warning notices from the RAF Commanding Officer forbidding access to certain areas where unstable explosives might still be buried. That was in 1985! Houses in Anglesey Road, Ash and Beech Street show signs of the damage caused in Burton on Trent, and many other such sites exist.

Horse and cart transport was widely used in Burton in the 1930s and 1940s. Domestic supplies including bread, milk and coal – each used the noble horse to deliver door to door. Breweries used these magnificent animals for a great variety of work including moving railway wagons by towing them along paved yards. In addition to all the usual building trades, Bass employed coppersmiths, tailors, blacksmiths, farriers, wheelwrights, coopers, platelayers, who laid and repaired the railway lines and one lone paviour who laid and relaid the granite setts which covered much of the brewery roads and yards. In my time this work was carried out by one man named Furniss, whose brother was a hairdresser in Horninglow Street, also a cricketer for Burton, and one of that rare breed, an independent councillor. Security employed many men whose chief officer was a Tom Walker who, it was said, had worked in the Royal Household. All watchmen wore the old type 'pill-box' peaked cap.

Wood Street, Burton, was bombed in, I believe, August 1940. We took cover in the shelter in Short Street School Yard. Our sleep was badly disturbed that night. Bus seats became wooden slats. Anderson shelters were built in some private gardens. Bluebell Wood is set back from the road opposite the 'A' Station gate of Drakelow Power Station. We cycled to pick bluebells only to find a sizable crater with masses of shrapnel, just inside the entrance. Nothing has been heard of that explosion, but it is quite conceivable that it was a shell from the 4.7in calibre naval guns which protected

Derby, fired at extreme range. The Burton public was invited to visit a hospital train parked in a sideline near No. 4 grain warehouse, while parked between the Ferry Bridge and the War Memorial was a Junkers aircraft with a very slim fuselage. This perhaps was the so-called 'Flying pencil'. It was gory to look at since congealed blood was still to be seen running from the crew positions!

Recruiting for the Burton Sea Cadet Unit took place at Goodman Street School, where I joined in 1942. Since everything was scarce at the time, things moved slowly. However when the unit moved to the rowing club premises in Stapenhill Road, a boom was provided to moor the first boat, which turned out to be an old ship's lifeboat, but nonetheless welcomed. 'Chains' were built where, unbelievably perhaps, we were taught to 'Swing the lead.' This was a heavy lead weight on a length of marked rope which swung ahead of a vessel would indicate the depth in fathoms (6§ft). Mark Twain is said to have been used as a pen-name by the author since he was a river pilot originally. 'By the mark twain' would have indicated two fathoms deep.

President of Burton Sea Cadet Unit was Lord Gretton of Bass, Ratcliff & Gretton. Commanding Officer was Lieutenant E. Tomlinson RNVR. First Lieutenant was Sub-Lt Hopcraft, and Sub-Lt Lake was Administrative Officer. Chief Petty Officer instructors included Harry Mann, Ted Lyons, Bob Woolley, Bill Coulton, Don Taylor and Reg Harrison. At a later stage we had a CPO Bandmaster from Winshill. These were experienced and dedicated men who contributed greatly to the success of the Burton Unit in addition to working full time at their workplace. They deserve recognition. Mr Taylor was a visual signals specialist, Reg Harrison was a radio amateur and taught that subject which included the Morse code (now officially declared redundant – a decision which will be regretted). In addition Reg coached the boxing team.

American troops were now ensconced in Burton. They all seemed enormously well off, with unlimited supplies of food and other desirables which they gave away most generously. Billeted mostly in disused malthouses, they had a huge open-air storage at Dixie sidings. Some were in the Territorial Army Centre in Horninglow Street, and I have an abiding memory of one black soldier guarding (notionally at least) a small entrance gate into the yard, which incidentally is still there today, with a rifle leaning against the door post and him leaning against the opposite post with a bag

of fish and chips which he was clearly enjoying. Visions of a British RSM's reaction to the scene remain with me still.

Bernard Davis, a railway engine driver and near neighbour of mine, passed an American soldier running across the Ferry Bridge pushing a child's push-chair with a safe onboard in the early hours of the day. The safe had been stolen from the Picturedrome cinema in Curzon Street earlier, but the soldier escaped detection until after the war.

Around thirty American soldiers, on an exercise, were attacking across the Leicester line railway between the Stapenhill footbridge , and the Rosliston Road bridge. Advancing down the cutting from Stapenhill, and charging up the other side into Drakelow, they were led by an officer wielding a sword. This took place in 1944. I cannot imagine he had landed on Omaha

Burton Sea Cadet officers, early 1940s. From left to right: Lt E. Tomlinson RNVR, Sub-Lt Hopcroft, CPO Coulton, Bandmaster Harry Mann, Ted Lyons, Sub-Lt Lake, Bob Woolley, Don Taylor. (H. Cox)

Burton Sea Cadets on parade.

Beach without more substantial armament.

Earlier in the war, Burton had been asked to adopt a warship for the Royal Navy. This we did, and the destroyer HMS *Savage* benefited. Her pennant number was G20; she took part in the battle of North Cape when the Home Fleet sank the German battleship *Scharnhorst*. The battle ensign worn by Savage in that action was presented to the town, and is displayed with the two plaques in the Council Chamber at Burton Town Hall.

Burton on Trent played its part to the full during the war; let us hope that we never experience such a time again.

Harold Cox

Stapenhill

My time at Stapenhill was special. In summer the days were long, hot and sunny and winters were cold and frosty, often with snow causing slides and snow fights on the way to school. The Second World War was only a rumble in the distance and at twelve years old the First World War was already in the history books with Wellington and Napoleon.

The lucky ones had dads who worked but many were unemployed and lived on a means test. There wasn't much left over to buy shoes and many survived with pieces of cardboard inside shoes to keep out the wet and cold. Some of us had bicycles – Hercules, Raleighs or ASPs (All Spare Parts).

We all seemed to be very patriotic and

on Empire Day many Union flags decorated our windows and at school a special play was put on bringing in all the countries of the Empire, on which we were told 'the sun never sets'. Many houses were still lit by gaslight and the 'privy' was at the bottom of the yard: a cold, dark trek on a winter's night. At school in housewifery we learnt to iron with a flat iron heated on the fire rubbed on emery cloth to smooth then onto candle grease to make it slide.

In autumn we looked forward to the clocks being put back. It meant darker nights and we could play foxes and hounds along Ferry Street or through the allotments. When this tired we would all gather round the gas street lamp, throw a rope over the top bar and take it in turns swinging round and round. Some of the lucky ones would have a penny to spend and we would all go to Hackett's fish and chip shop for a bag of chips – the favoured ones able to beg a few.

The gas lighter came along at dusk with a hook on a pole to light up the gas mantle from the pilot light, always left on. He must have walked many miles each day.

The local doctor was a Dr Thompson. Not many of us knew him except by name because a visit cost half a crown. We were dosed at home with possibly a pennyworth of ipecacuanha bought from the corner shop or in the spring with a spoonful of brimstone and treacle to cleanse the blood.

Living at the corner shop brought some rewards but also some extra tasks. Sugar was delivered in hundredweight sacks and had to be weighed out into blue 2lb sugar bags, my job. I often had to cycle to various wholesalers to bring back emergency supplies of sausage, sometimes butter and sometimes cigarettes. We opened at 7 a.m. and many workmen used to come into the shop for their day's ration of cigarettes —

Empire Day, 1932. (M. Browne)

Party given to Stapenhill children at the chapel room. (M. Browne)

The opening of the Ferry Bridge by Lord Burton.

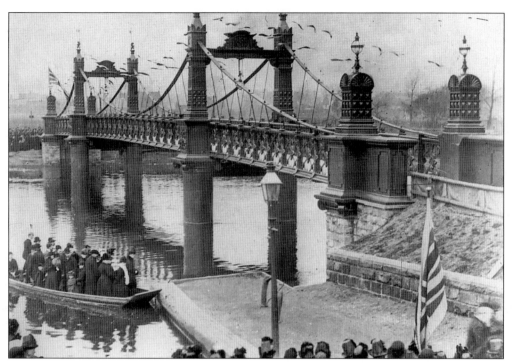

The very last ferry crossing.

five woodbines for twopence. The rich ones would call in the evening on their way home for a further five.

Stapenhill House was still standing in 1931, the home of Miss Goodger. I attended St Peter's School opposite the house (it is now a doctor's practice). The daughter of the caretaker of Stapenhill House was a friend of mine, Brenda Orton, and we often used to play on the roof of the house. It was a splendid place with some flat roof and some huge chimneys. Miss Goodger was the first woman Mayor of Burton and when she died she left her house and garden to the people of Burton. This wonderful gift is now enjoyed by so many Burtonians as Stapenhill Gardens.

In 1932 my mother decided to give a party for local Stapenhill children. Many of the wholesalers donated foods like butter,

sugar, bread and sweets. The local chapel room was booked and several adults worked hard organizing the event with enthusiasm. Two teachers arranged the games and Pirelli supplied lots of balloons. Much cooking was done and a good time was had by all. Seventy children came.

September 1933 saw me running across the Ferry Bridge to continue my education at Guild Street School. Discipline was so strict. Woebetide an unfortunate girl sent to Miss McGregor's room for a wrongdoing. We were surprised (and some of us confused) when we were taught the Pythagoras theorem. We sometimes feared Miss Press who often shouted, 'How can I be expected to teach you French grammar when you don't understand English grammar?'

In 1934 Sir Alan Cobham came to

Burton. He offered trips in his aeroplane around the Burton area for ten shillings (a great deal at the time). The Burton *Mail* ran a competition. If you could spot the deliberate mistake in the paper a free trip was yours. (In those days there was seldom an accidental error in a newspaper.) My Mother spotted the mistake and the free trip was ours. It was much enjoyed, much feared and of course I was the envy of my fellow pupils. I had permission to be absent from school. My mother wrote that flying would be an education and justified time off from lessons.

Our King died in 1936 and there was much mourning. The Prince of Wales was proclaimed King Edward VIII. In Burton the Proclamation took place at the Town Hall and I believe hardly any of the public were there to listen. A quick message was sent to our school: 'Send some pupils here quickly'. We wore green pork pie pull-on hats with a silver badge. To be caught in the street hatless was a crime, which merited the worst punishment.

I left school and left Burton in 1937 to go to Nottingham. There begins another story.

Marian Browne

Tatenhill

At Tatenhill post office a hundred years ago the day began early with the arrival of the mail from the Head Post Office at Burton-on-Trent. May Shipley first assisted in the post office. She later took over as postmistress. While the letters and packages were being sorted May would send Amy, the

Tatenhill School children with Miss Wilkins, 1906/07. (K. Young)

Thomas Shipley at work about 1895 (K. Young)

eldest daughter living at home, out to the paddock at the side of the post office to harness Maggie the cob horse into the trap which would be used to take the mail to outlying villages. When the trap was ready Amy's next task was to deliver the mail to Postern House, then she would cut across the fields to leave any mail at the gamekeepers' bothy in Knightley Woods. On her way to Postern House Amy would leave a milk can at Pool Green Farm, collecting it full of fresh milk on her way home.

May Shipley's husband, Thomas Shipley, was the village blacksmith, a business he had taken over from his father, William Shipley. The forge was at the top of Mill Lane. As well as shoeing horses and repairing carts Thomas Shipley did wrought-iron work including work for the screen in Hoar Cross church. In the 'season' he made iron hoops for children to bowl along the road.

As well as being a blacksmith Thomas Shipley was also sexton of St Michael & All Angels' church. The children were involved in some aspects of this work. On the day of a funeral the children might be sent with a long-handled ladle to bale out water from the bottom of the open grave. They would then break off branches from the trees to line the bottom of the grave. Amy would fetch a hammer from her father's forge, climb the ladders into the bell loft of the church and strike the clock bell with a sequence of three strokes for a man, two for a woman, one for a child. Amy would keep watch through the window of the church tower and, as the cortège approached she would quicken the pace of the strokes to alert the mourners already in the church.

Kathleen Young

Coronation Celebrations At Wychnor

On 22 January 1901 the Victorian era closed with the death of the Queen after a reign of 63 years. The following day her eldest son Edward made his accession speech and on 24 January the column inches of the Burton Chronicle were edged in black as a sign of mourning and respect with the inside pages giving a detailed account of Victoria's life. On Friday 25 January the proclamation of the accession of Edward VII to the throne was made at St James Palace in London and simultaneously at provincial locations, one of them being by the Mayor of Lichfield outside the Guildhall. Ten days later on 2 February Queen Victoria's state funeral took place. There followed a period of mourning so that the proposed date for the coronation of Edward VII was the following year on 26 June 1902.

The people of the village of Wychnor had plenty of time to plan what they would do to celebrate the coronation. They, like many other small country communities, had few opportunities for celebrations other than those attached to church festivals or the occasional wedding so this was going to be a big occasion requiring careful preparation. The first step was to form a committee. They held their first meeting in the Wychnor schoolroom in mid-May. In the chair was Mr W.S. Shaw, also present were Mr S.H. Shaw who acted as secretary, the three local farmers Messrs. Blant, Potter and Shuker, and the estate bailiff from Wychnor Park, William Smith.

To finance the festivities they opened a subscription list with Basil Levett the owner of Wychnor Park starting the ball rolling with the sum of £10, the three farmers contributed £1 5s, but most of the other contributions reflected the restricted means of the farm labourers, canal or railway workers who contributed between two 2s 6d and 6d depending on what they could afford. Miss Gillingham the school teacher felt able to give 10s. In all £24 18s 3d was raised for the village celebration.

It was decided that there should be a service in the church, all of the children should be presented with a commemorative mug, sports events would be held, a bonfire and fireworks and of course, refreshments. The meat was to be ordered from Coates butchers in Alrewas. Mr Potter and Mr Blant were to provide the milk and Mr Newton the potatoes. Mr Potter and Mr Blant were also to look for musicians to provide entertainment on the day.

At the second meeting of the committee on Saturday 7 June Mr Potter reported that he had secured the services of musicians under the direction of Mr Lindop of Barton, on favourable terms. He also reported that the ladies associated with the committee had arranged to provide other provisions such as tea, sugar, cakes bread and butter and that Mrs Potter had agreed to cook the meat assisted by Mrs Moore who would be cooking the hams. Mr Potter was then asked to order the supplies of ginger beer, lemonade and ginger ale that he thought would be necessary for the occasion. For the men who would be attending Mr Blant was asked to purchase 3lbs of tobacco in half-ounces, to be distributed by him on Coronation day. The secretary was asked to find out for the next meeting how many people would actually be attending.

The next meeting convened on Friday 13 June when Mr Potter was able to report that the arrangements had been made for the supply of ginger beer, lemonade and the mugs for the children. He had also made arrangements with the vicar from Alrewas, Revd W.A. Webb as to the time of the Coronation service. With this vital piece of information they were able to draw up a programme for the day.

12.00 p.m. Special Coronation Service in the church.
1.00 p.m. Dinner
2.30 p.m. onwards Sports
4.30 p.m. Tea for the women and children
6.00 p.m. Presentation of Mugs
6.30 p.m. onwards Dancing
Dusk Bonfire and Fireworks.

It was agreed that Mrs Potter be asked to present the mugs to the children but the secretary asked that the names of the children who were to receive mugs should be given to him before the day.

Since there were to be sports, a sports committee was proposed. This had Mr Blant as chairman with Messrs Shuker, Newton, G. Potter, W. Potter and S.H. Shaw to help him, and they were allowed £2 out of the funds for prizes. The final decisions involved staff from the Wychnor Park Estate where the Estate Baliff Mr Smith and Mr Sam Wassell the head woodman were asked to see to the bonfire and Mr Bates was asked to provide seating and tables for 170 people.

Everything was now in a state of preparation with everyone knowing what they had to do ready for the celebration that was a fortnight away. There was a state of heightened expectation added to by the Burton Chronicle which for weeks had filled pages with Coronation items about regalia, ceremonial, who would be present in Westminster Abbey and so on. There were detailed lithographic drawings of the decorated buildings in Burton (no photographs), and reports from around the villages of their preparations for the great day. It was announced that Friday 25 June the day after the Coronation was to be a bank holiday. To add to the excitement thanksgiving services were being held as a result of the ending of the Boer War in South Africa and the final surrender of Boer forces on 16 June.

In the Burton Chronicle of 22 June concern was expressed about the health of the King. On 25 June it was announced that the King had been operated on to remove his appendix the day before and that the Coronation was to be postponed. An additional announcement stated that the King was aware that many festivities around the country had been arranged for the Coronation and that it was his wish that they should go ahead on the planned day if the organisers so wished. The Wychnor committee quickly convened and decided that they would hold over the celebrations for a month and even though a rearranged date had not been announced for the Coronation decided to hold the local celebrations Saturday 26 July.

After the church service and the dinner the company assembled on Mr Blant's field for the sports, some of them taken more seriously than others. The first event was the 80 yard race for men over forty, five of the local community took off their jackets and crouched at the line to be sent on their way by the starter Mr Blant. Alfred Breeze took the first prize of a spade, Charles Woodings gained a hoe for coming second as did George Wagg for coming third.

The second race was over 100 yards for farm men under the age of forty. For the five starters pride and prestige was more of an issue than the prizes at the end. G.H. Bentley gained a fork for coming first while

J. Copeland and W. James gained hoes for coming second and third. The open 100 yard race which followed had nine starters and was a much more serious affair with the 3s first prize – the equivalent of a day's pay – just for a fifteen seconds dash. Fred Paine took the honours with Ernest Kay being the runner-up with a prize of 2s, Joseph Dickenson was awarded 1s for coming third. There were two 100 yard races for the boys, one for the under eighteens and the other for boys still at school. Here the prizes were the much sought after clasp knives. George Kay distinguished himself by coming third in the first race and then first in the race for the boys still attending school. Two pocket knives made him the envy of many of his school classmates.

The sports now took on a more light hearted tone as five married women lined up for their 80 yard race. Hats, coats and shawls discarded they seemed almost to glide over the grass in their ankle length full dresses. Selina Woolley's prize for coming first was an alarm clock while Mrs Partridge went home with six spoons and the third placed Mrs Weate took home a handicraft box. There then followed two rounds of a Tug of War between four teams of five a side, the winning team being rewarded with one shilling each. There was a sack race which stated that it was open entry but the gardening tools as prizes indicated that it was really for men. There followed a variety of races for younger children, and the 100 yard race for single women. Laura Partridge took home a cruet set for coming first while Annie Barker gained six spoons and Lucy Stacke had 1s for coming third. No doubt the first two prizes would have been added to items already gathered in a 'bottom drawer'.

The races over there was tea for the women and children at 4.30 p.m., since there was no provision in the programme for the men to have tea they probably went away to enjoy their pipes with the ounces of tobacco provided out of the funds. At six 6.00 p.m. Mrs Potter presented souvenir mugs to the school children after which Mr Lindop provided the music for dancing. As dusk fell the bonfire assembled by Mr Wassell was lit and sparks flew up into the darkening sky. It was decided that it was not appropriate in the circumstances to use the fireworks that had been purchased at cost of £1. Standing round watching the leaping flames were young couples holding hands, family groups with tired young children, lads stirring the fire to make it blaze more fiercely and the older ones just sitting in quiet contemplation, for all of them it would be a day to remember. For even the oldest, the last coronation was so long ago that it was beyond the recall of memory. Gradually as the fire turned to embers the watchers made their way home.

The following Monday there was a meeting of the Coronation festivities committee when the accounts were submitted. Mr Potter the treasurer reported that there was a surplus balance of £4 11s 8d. It was agreed by the meeting to use the balance towards any further Coronation festivities on 9 August, which had been announced as the new date for the coronation.

On Sunday 3 August Wychnor had another event to excite the people. The Vicar of Alrewas Revd W.A. Webb was to be installed as the new Vicar of Wychnor, with the Bishop of Lichfield in attendance to perform the installation. During the service the bishop unveiled a memorial window dedicated to the memory of the late Colonel Theophilus John Levett, presented to the

Sports Prizes

26th July 1902

Race		First	Second	Third
80 yards for Men over 40 years of Age				
	Alfred Breeze	Spade		
	Charles Woodings		Hoe	
	George Wagg			Hoe
	5 Starters.			
Race. 100 yds. for Farm Men under 40 years of Age				
	G. H. Bentley	Fork		
	J. Copeland		Hoe	
	W. James			Hoe
	5 Starters			
Race. 100 yards. Open.				
	Fred Paine	3/-		
	Ernest Kay		2/-	
	Joseph Dickenson			1/-
	9 Starters			
Race. 100 yds. for Boys under 18 years of Age				
	Fred Kay	Knife		
	Walter Breeze		Knife	
	George Kay			Knife
	11 Starters.			

117

church by Lady Jane Levett.

On Saturday 9 August the delayed Coronation took place in London and the Coronation Festivities Committee rounded off the Wychnor celebrations by providing a tea for all the women and children of the parish with a supper for the men. This used up the balance of the money, which had been added to by a £1 10s 11d of subscriptions. While the committee undoubtedly felt satisfied that they had completed their task successfully they were not to know that they would be called on to repeat their activities nine years later for the Coronation of King George V.

My thanks are due to Mrs Margaret Stanhope for access to the Minutes and Accounts of the Wychnor Coronation Festivities Committee. Roger Hailwood.

Roger Hailwood

Whispers in Yoxall

Yoxall – the village that's always in my heart. The village where generations of my family have lived. These days Yoxall is expanding more and more each day, with its inhabitants multiplying, new houses and estates built and a whisper of a bypass to build and split the original village in two. This is large in comparison to what it used to be, one main street leading all the way from the Trent Bridge to Hadley End.

My family are the Smiths of Yoxall. Although they are not the oldest family from the village they are well known and have a terrific history. A lot of the older names of the village were used as street names when the estate was built. Jane Austen used to visit her cousins in the village, the Coopers. Edward Cooper was the rector of the parish from 1809 until 1833. Also the author Izaak Walton's father, George Walton, used to live at Birmingham House, now known as No. 1 King Street or the antique shop.

Another well-known name of the village are the Ardens. The Arden family lived at Longcroft Hall, which was sadly demolished. Mary Arden was the mother of William Shakespeare. William used to travel to Yoxall to visit his cousin, Simon Arden, the son of Emily Jane, Mary's sister. They lived in The Hollies, the three-storey house on the main road. Emily married Michael Bass, who became the parents of Michael Arthur Bass, the 1 Baron of Burton.

In 1904 they laid the foundation stone for Yoxall Parish Hall. The Baroness returned to open the hall on 2 August 1905. Lady Burton also opened the cheese factory in 1906. The factory was situated halfway between the Trent Bridge and Bond End, now known as Leavlite Anodising. The cheese factory was part of the Yoxall dairy farmers who bought the factory in the late nineteenth century as a cottage and adapted it by adding buildings. The business later failed. It was sold and used as a private house.

This is where James Berrisford Smith lived until he died on 11 November 1935. Leavlite Anodising opened in the early 1970s. My granddad, Thomas Henry Smith, worked at Leavlite until he retired. He heard a rumour of a ghost in the factory. It remained a rumour until one of his friends was spooked one night in the canteen, which was situated at the front of the buildings, part of the original cottage. When explaining his experience, he described a well-built man, with white hair and tash, a hat, with a butcher's apron on. This is an identical description to Thomas's granddad, James Berrisford Smith.

James moved to the cottage from Swarbourn House, on the corner of Ferrers Road and next door to the Crown. This was the Smiths' family house for many years. James was a skilled butcher. The slaughterhouse was a building still attached to the house. In the roof is a large wooden wheel, approximately 3ft 6in in diameter, the axle running on leather bearings, together with the remains of a block and tackle for hoisting the animal and the wall part of the device for holding the animal's head. Three generations of Smiths lived here. The fields behind the house were later sold for the new project of a housing estate.

James' parents were Harriet and Alfred Smith. They married in 1863 at St. Peters Church, Yoxall and owned a farm in Anslow. Alfred came from a farm in Abbots Bromley, son of John Smith. Harriet's father was James Berrisford. He came back to Yoxall after retiring as a prize fighter. His occupation in the 1881 Census was butcher and beerhouse keeper at the Shoulder of Mutton. This was situated on the corner of Hadley Street, opposite the post office. If you look carefully you can still see where the sign was for the public house. Also in the 1881 Census it states that James Berrisford had an apprentice butcher living with him, his grandson, James Berrisford Smith , aged seventeen.

James Berrisford Smith was later

The sign for the Tatenhill post office can just be seen over the furthest door facing the road.

James Berrisford Smith. (C. Butler)

married to Mary Elizabeth. They had eight children. The eldest was called James Berrisford. (It becomes very confusing when succeeding generations used to call their eldest son James. A lot of families used to pass on their name in this way.) He emigrated to America to become a cowboy, then was later ordained and returned to Staffordshire to become the vicar of Denstone. James and Mary's fourth child was William Henry, the father of Thomas.

William was born 2 January 1895, he weighed 14lbs, the heaviest baby the doctor had ever seen. He served in the First World War. For a while he was a Grenadier, guarding Buckingham Palace, but during the war, he was saved by his bandoleer, when hit by shrapnel. He kept the bullet that saved his life for proof. After the war he met and married Lillian Moore; they had six children together. Sadly Lillian died shortly after the birth of their youngest child in 1939. William carried on loving and supporting his family. He carried on the family line of butchering, and during the Second World War he worked in Branston, Burton, with the only means of travel over the eleven miles being on foot. William also made the papers in 1986, when the Burton Mail interviewed him for being the oldest man in Yoxall at the age of ninety-two.

Claire Butler

Fred's Snippet

Mrs Auden lived at the Poplars in Rolleston Road. Her family built Horninglow church. Every Christmas we would go and sing carols to Mrs Auden and she would sit there in Victorian frocks. We were given a mince pie for singing. I was a bellringer at Horninglow church for seventeen years. I had No. 4 bell. It was cracked, you know. I think the vicar was Revd Spinney. He had come there after his marriage and his wife was expecting a baby. When the baby was born, he fetched us six bellringers into the vicarage to celebrate the birth of a daughter and got us all drunk. The first person to be buried in the church yard was Eliza Turner. She is in a crypt at the left of the entrance to the church.

A tradition no longer with us. (F. Smith)

The cedar tree at Bretby Hall, owned by Lord Stanhope. Gypsies put a spell on it and said that if ever a branch fell off someone would die in the family so Lord Stanhope had chains put on the branches to hold them up. (F. Smith)

CHAPTER 8
Picture the Past

Amongst the submitted pieces received there were many extra interesting photographs. Although they did not correspond directly to the content of the entries, it was thought that they might stir some dormant memory, from the Queen's visit to the familiar face of John Jennings MP. A more recent event as the building of St Peter's Bridge and the opening was captured by Mr R. Tipper of Stapenhill to one of the most photographed places in Burton, the white swan and surroundings in Stapenhill Gardens.

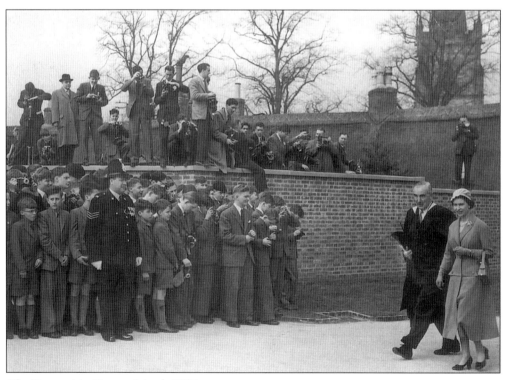

The Queen visits Repton, March 1957.

The Queen calls at Tutbury.

John Jennings MP with John Rose, secretary of the regatta, queries the 'foam' on the river.

Have you noticed at the corner of New Street and High Street there are two brass L's set in the road? That was where the old Gatehouse to the Abbey stood. (F. Smith)

A long load trying to negotiate the turning from High Street into Horninglow Street.

The Saracen's Head Inn is now part of the Queens Hotel

Building St Peter's Bridge in the snow. (R. Tipper)

The opening of St Peter's Bridge and the first crossing, 30 June 1985. (R. Tipper)

Stapenhill Pleasure Gardens.

A view down Station Street, with the Roebuck Inn on the right. The buildings in view are all still standing.

Ind Coope loading bay. No pneumatic tyres yet.

The level crossing at Station Street. Two crossing men wait in the box, ready to open the gates.